In addition to her research in Anglo-Irish literature, *Carol Kleiman* teaches English at the University of Manitoba and the University of Winnipeg.

In this innovative study, Carol Kleiman reassesses in a practical way O'Casey's contribution to modern drama. The four interrelated essays show how his plays bridge two radically experimental theatres: the Expressionist and the Absurd. It is from this vantage point, this 'bridge of vision,' that the entire O'Casey canon can be viewed in a new perspective.

Set in this larger critical compass, the relation between his two great visionary plays, *The Silver Tassie* and *Red Roses for Me*, so central to O'Casey's work, reveals both the scope of his vision and the complex nature of his developing craftsmanship. In addition, Kleiman is able to suggest the intriguing possibility of solving the *Silver Tassie* controversy on the contemporary stage. Not only does this study provide practical suggestions for stage production, it also points to profitable avenues for future critical investigation.

'It is high time for critics to get away from the present overemphasis on O'Casey's characterization and to pay attention, as Carol Kleiman does with intelligence and sensitivity, to dramatic structure and theatrical presentation. These four essays throw new light on important aspects of the two plays and upon O'Casey's creative affinities with significant Expressionist and Absurdist writers.' Ronald Ayling, University of Alberta.

CAROL KLEIMAN

Sean O'Casey's Bridge of Vision: Four Essays on Structure and Perspective

UNIVERSITY OF TORONTO PRESS
Toronto Buffalo London

©University of Toronto Press 1982
Toronto Buffalo London
Printed in Canada

ISBN 0-8020-2431-9

Canadian Cataloguing in Publication Data

Kleiman, Carol J.
Sean O'Casey's bridge of vision
Bibliography: p.
Includes index.
ISBN 0-8020-2431-9

1. O'Casey, Sean, 1880–1964 – Criticism and
interpretation – Addresses, essays, lectures.
2. O'Casey, Sean, 1880–1964. The silver tassie.
3. O'Casey, Sean, 1880–1964. Red roses for me.
I. Title.
PR6029.C33Z72   822'.912   C81-095141-X

COVER: O'Connell Bridge, Dublin. *Courtesy of the National Library of Ireland, Dublin*

FRONTISPIECE: Sean and Eileen O'Casey leaving the Church of Our Most Holy Redeemer and St Thomas More, Chelsea, London, after their marriage on 23 September 1927. *Private collection.* O'Casey was writing *The Silver Tassie*, his most satirical and despairing play, at the time when – courting his 'lovely and darling Eily' – he was most happy. *The Tassie* is dedicated to 'Eileen with the yellow daffodils in the green vase.'

This book has been published with the help of grants from the Canadian Federation for the Humanities, using funds provided by the Social Sciences and Humanities Research Council of Canada, and from the Publications Fund of the University of Toronto Press.

For Ed

Who through every inch of life weaves a patthern of vigour an' elation can never taste death, but goes to sleep among th' stars ...

Red Roses for Me

Contents

Acknowledgements

Passages from the following works are reprinted by permission of the publishers: Sean O'Casey's *Collected Plays, The Drums of Father Ned, The Moon Shines on Kylenamoe, Under a Colored Cap, Blasts and Benedictions* (selected and introduced by Ronald Ayling), published by Macmillan, London and Basingstoke, and by St Martin's Press, Inc., New York; O'Casey's *The Silver Tassie* and *Red Roses for Me* (first editions), the autobiography of Sean O'Casey, *Mirror in My House*, and *The Sting and the Twinkle: Conversations with Sean O'Casey* (edited by E.H. Mikhail and John O'Riordan), published by Macmillan, London and Basingstoke; O'Casey's *The Green Crow*, published by George Braziller, Inc., New York; *Mirror in My House* and *The Letters of Sean O'Casey* (edited by David Krause), published by Macmillan Publishing Co., Inc., New York.

For permission to quote from the holographs and typescripts of *The Silver Tassie* in the Henry W. and Albert A. Berg Collection, and for permission to reproduce the holographs, I would like to thank the New York Public Library (Astor, Lenox and Tilden Foundations) and Eileen O'Casey. I am especially indebted to Mrs O'Casey, whose gracious responses to my inquiries, on several occasions, have been most helpful.

Part of Chapter 1 appeared in *The Canadian Journal of Irish Studies* (Vol. v, June 1979), edited by Dr Andrew Parkin; and an earlier version of Chapter 4 appeared in *The Sean O'Casey Review: An International Journal of O'Casey Studies* (Vol. IV, Spring 1978), edited by Robert G. Lowery. I am grateful to both editors for permission to republish.

I am indebted to Raymond Massey for permission to quote from our correspondence, and for permission to reproduce his letter from Sean O'Casey.

Dr Konrad Gross, of the University of Kiel, has been very helpful in obtaining various research materials for me in both Dublin and West Germany and I would like to thank him here.

I would also like to express my appreciation to Dr Fahmy Farag, of the University of Winnipeg, for reading and commenting on an earlier version of the manuscript.

Finally, I would like to thank Dr Walter Swayze, of the University of Winnipeg, who kept telling me that *Sean O'Casey's Bridge of Vision* had to be written and who, while 'crossing' and 'recrossing' it with me in the earliest manuscript version, made many valuable suggestions for revision.

Introduction:
Bridging the River of Time

'This is O'Casey's *apotheosis*,'[1] Yeats cried at the time of the riots over *The Plough and the Stars*, and Sean O'Casey – so the story goes – ran home to look up the word in the dictionary. In 1928, however, when Yeats led the other Abbey Theatre directors in rejecting the radically experimental *Silver Tassie*, O'Casey did not need a dictionary to tell him what the rejection meant. Once more, an oracular voice had spoken (or so it seemed), and O'Casey was, for the time being, hurled from his brief sojourn among the stars.

Thus began the much-publicized *Silver Tassie* controversy, which for decades kept O'Casey's later plays from the stage, while proclaiming the Dublin trilogy – *Shadow of a Gunman, Juno and the Paycock, The Plough* – to be the true measure of his success for all time. O'Casey, of course, could not agree. He was reported to be 'sick' of people talking about *Juno*: 'it was a good enough play for a man just beginning,' he explained, 'but no more than that.'[2] Here, hidden within this somewhat enigmatic statement, O'Casey expresses his intense longing for the revaluation of *The Tassie*, which, throughout his lifetime, he believed to be his unacknowledged masterpiece.

And yet, unlikely as it would have seemed then, this revaluation, which could well alter our whole way of looking at his work, has been, for some time now, 'in the air.' The kind of scholarly attention being given O'Casey at present – the founding, for example, of *The Sean O'Casey Review*,[3] edited by Robert G. Lowery and contributed to by dedicated O'Casey scholars everywhere – is gradually providing a more favourable climate for the reassessment of the individual plays. Indeed, such in-depth studies as David Krause has long been calling for could well result in a reassessment of O'Casey's historical significance as a major dramatist of the twentieth century. For O'Casey is not only a prolific and visionary writer, he is also a master craftsman of the theatre whose relationship to his contemporaries and to present-day dramatists is finally beginning to be discerned.

No complete 're-viewing' of O'Casey can take place, however, so long as the *Silver Tassie* controversy continues to bar the way, obscuring, as it does, the true nature of O'Casey's innovative, and visionary, craftsmanship. This book, in attempting to resolve that controversy and so create a new context for O'Casey, examines the charges brought against the play by Yeats and tests them out against the complex structure of the play itself.

In this process, within the brilliant spectrum of the later plays, there is an unexpected ally: *The Tassie*'s 'mirror twin,' *Red Roses for Me*. Together, these two plays explore the outermost reaches of man's vision: downward into the abyss and upward to that final transfiguration 'among th' stars.'[4] But it is their complex interrelationship that reveals the full extent of O'Casey's skill in the development of his craft; for he is able to span these vast distances in the twinkling of an eye, while, at the same time, maintaining a strong sense of both an inner and an outer reality. In fact, to explore in detail the interrelated structure of these two great visionary plays is to go straight to the heart of the matter: the enigmatic *Silver Tassie* controversy and the intriguing possibility of its 'solution' on our own contemporary stage.

But this solution cannot occur overnight. Rather, it must be part of an ongoing critical process which involves readers, students, scholars, reviewers, directors, actors, and audience alike. For this reason, and in the hope of solving those special problems encountered by two plays which are ambitious enough to present visions onstage, I have included, in an appendix, detailed notes for production.

Coming to grips with the problem of how these visionary plays might be staged should also help to clarify and confirm O'Casey's stature as a dramatic craftsman whose work bridges two experimental theatres: the Expressionist and the Absurd. Conversely, an understanding of O'Casey's immediate historical context, which ranges from the theatre of Strindberg and Toller to that of Beckett and Ionesco, helps to illuminate the innovative stagecraft of the plays themselves. My own discovery of such a context began with the text of *Red Roses for Me*, with the mask-like faces, the ritualized processions, the choral speeches, all of which led backward to Expressionism, to O'Casey's first clearly 'expressionist' play, *The Silver Tassie*, and then ahead, surprisingly, to the Theatre of the Absurd.

Thus, stretching across the River of Time itself, the 'bridge of vision' which Ayamonn crosses in the third act of *Red Roses for Me* becomes, finally, a metaphor which is central to O'Casey's life and art. And from this Bridge of Vision it is possible to gain a new perspective on the plays from *The Silver Tassie* onward, as well as a new perspective on O'Casey's place in the development of the modern drama.

Accordingly, the first chapter looks at the extent to which O'Casey is indebted to such dramatists as Strindberg and Toller in order to check the growing tendency to exaggerate O'Casey's debt to continental Expressionism. Unquestionably, O'Casey did employ certain carefully chosen techniques of expressionism; still others he assimilated unconsciously. But he continually used these techniques in a highly individual way to express his own tragi-comic vision of man, a vision which always involves his awareness of the 'humanly absurd.'⁵ The concluding chapter, then, looks at O'Casey's work in relation to the Theatre of the Absurd, a theatre whose debt to the revolutionary experiments of Sean O'Casey is just beginning to be recognized. In this new context, at the centre of the book, are the studies of the visionary plays.

When scenes from *The Siver Tassie* and *Red Roses for Me* are looked at, first in the light of Expressionism, and then in the light of the Absurd, those two opposing sides of man's humanity – his idealism and his absurdity – both of which O'Casey loved, and loved to laugh at, spring into a clear relief. Yet, if the vogue of the Absurd, like that of Expressionism, should die away, O'Casey will remain, since in his plays we can discern those timeless qualities which these two radically experimental theatres have brought into such sharp focus.

Clearly, the broadest perspective which these visionary plays invite is that afforded, not only by Expressionism and the Theatre of the Absurd, but also by the mystery and morality plays of the Middle Ages, when, as O'Casey wrote in 'Behind the Curtained World,' the theatre 'had a big life and a gorgeous time ... showing the goodness of God and the evil of Satan to the gaping crowds.'⁶ In *The Second Shepherds' Play*, the broad farce of Mak hiding the stolen sheep in an infant's cradle on the morning of Christ's nativity contains perhaps as concrete a statement about the nature of the divine comedy as anyone could wish for. Similarly, the tossing of Mak in a blanket as punishment for the theft (which was usually punished by hanging) contains an instructive commentary on the redemptive nature of man.

It is in the historical context of this broader tradition, where the absurd and the miraculous, the grotesque and the sublime go hand in hand (as they did in the little stable at Bethlehem) that *The Silver Tassie* and *Red Roses for Me* demand, finally, to be understood. For, paradoxically, in an age where, as both O'Casey and the absurdists knew, 'God is dead' (*RR* 151), these two great visionary plays remain among the more moving embodiments of that ancient mystery of sacrifice and redemption, translated into contemporary terms, that the twentieth century has produced.

SEAN O'CASEY'S BRIDGE OF VISION

1

O'Casey's 'Homemade' Expressionism: His Debt to Toller

The label 'Expressionist,' as Eric Bentley points out, was originally stuck on O'Casey in order to discredit his work. It was a term of disapprobation meant to suggest that 'he read books by foreign authors or spent his holidays beyond the Rhine,' as well as to 'intimat[e] that his later style was not his own.'[1] Though this particular type of non-literary criticism is no longer in vogue either in North America or elsewhere, its heritage lies in an occasional tendency to refer to certain of O'Casey's plays – *The Star Turns Red, Red Roses for Me* – as the 'Red' plays, a category which is as misleading as it is superficial in the values it suggests. For what both these plays tell us is that communism, to O'Casey, means 'communion,' and the bread it gives to the worker becomes, ideally, the bread of the eucharist – an unusual translation for one who proclaimed himself to be both communist and atheist.

Still, the label 'Expressionist' – now divorced from the implicit stigma of the label 'Red' – has stuck, and the interest in this particular aspect of O'Casey's work continues to grow. However, as critics turned away from berating O'Casey for his so-called Expressionism and for refusing to return to his 'early' manner, a new problem arose. If his 'later' manner is to be thought of, not as some wild and perverse aberration from the course of his true genius, but as a natural and spontaneous development of a maturing talent, then how was the apparent stylistic break in the O'Casey canon to be understood? How was the apparently vast gulf in terms of technique which seemed to exist between the early plays of the Dublin trilogy and those plays from *The Silver Tassie* onward to be explained?

In some of his own critical writings O'Casey gives us the answers, though these have been as frequently misinterpreted as understood. For example, in 'Green Goddess of Realism' he brilliantly debunks what William Archer calls 'verisimilitude – the genius of the commonplace':

> This rage for real, real life on the stage has taken all the life out of the drama. If everything on the stage is to be a fake exact imitation (for fake realism it can only be), where is the chance for the original and imaginative artist? Less chance for him than there was for Jonah in the whale's belly. The beauty, fire, and poetry of drama have perished in the storm of fake realism. Let real birds fly through the air ... real animals roam through the jungle, real fish swim in the sea; but let us have the make-believe of the artist and the child in the theatre. Less of what the critics call 'life,' and more of symbolism; for even in the most commonplace of realistic plays the symbol can never be absent. A house on a stage can never be a house, and that which represents it must always be a symbol. A room in a realistic play must always be a symbol for a room.[2]

In this plea for expanding imaginatively the limits of the realistic stage, a plea in defence of his own developing work that he was to make many times in different ways throughout his lifetime, O'Casey asks for more symbolism in the theatre, and for more make-believe. Here, then, are those magical qualities which, together with his 'communism,' help to account for the term 'Expressionist' being used in connection with his work. Yet it may well be only in the context of O'Casey's complex realistic and symbolic structures, rather than in the context of a nebulous, sometimes insulting, and often exaggerated Expressionism that we can discern the most basic links between the Dublin trilogy and the later plays.

In his foreword to *The Green Crow* O'Casey explains that his 'first play ever to appear in print was in his later manner.'[3] He is referring to *Roisin's Robe*, printed in *The Plain People* years before *The Shadow of a Gunman* appeared, and he speaks also of *Kathleen Listens In*, the satirical fantasy that was written after *Shadow of a Gunman*, though both were produced in the same year (1923). *Roisin's Robe* has unfortunately been lost,[4] but anyone who has read *Kathleen* will recognize at once the validity of O'Casey's own critical judgement. There is certainly a much greater affinity between this early work of O'Casey's and his own later work (especially those plays written after the 'middle' years) than there is between his later works and the plays of the Expressionist stage.

CONTINENTAL EXPRESSIONISM VS 'HOMEMADE'

Yet there are few critics who have been able to discern what Eric Bentley realized long ago: the continental Expressionism of Strindberg or Toller is quite different from the 'homemade' expressionism of Sean O'Casey. When this latter term is used it is also easier to keep in mind the curious O'Casey temperament in which, as Harold Clurman says, 'there is a drive towards cosmic grandeur and a persistent village homeliness.'[5] Nor are we so likely to forget that O'Casey's 'cosmically' comic vision could only view the usually unrelieved seriousness of the German Expressionists, despite certain affinities in outlook, with obvious reservations. O'Casey does, of course, owe a debt to the Expressionists – mainly to Ernst Toller – but it is a debt that has often become so exaggerated by detractors and admirers alike that it has cost him dearly to repay.

Many confusing connotations could, in fact, be avoided if a clearer distinction were made between 'Expressionism' as an art form strongly imbued with certain ideological beliefs and 'expressionism' understood simply as an artistic technique. To speak of O'Casey as an 'Expressionist' and to liken his work without qualification to Toller's, as critics have done, is really to place O'Casey in a context where he does not belong and to make an anachronism of his work. Such a viewing also reinforces the erroneous notion that a good part of his later work is propaganda, and that his self-exile from Ireland forced him to turn for inspiration from the rich tradition of realism and naturalism fostered by the Abbey Theatre to the experiments of foreign dramatists. Though there is a special kinship with Toller which has yet to be recognized and which needs to be more fully explored, it can be confusing even to speak of O'Casey as a dramatist who uses various techniques of expressionism if one begins to assume that these techniques, as O'Casey uses them, have very much in common with the work, say, of Strindberg or Wedekind.[6]

For example, if we look at the fluid, 'kaleidoscopic' effect that Strindberg creates in *A Dream Play* (such as the scene outside the Portress' window changing before our very eyes into an attorney's office), then we should become aware of how different this succession of short scenes is in comparison with the carefully structured acts and quite concrete stage settings of an O'Casey play. Even in the second act of *The Silver Tassie* and the third act of *Red Roses for Me*, habitually thought of as completely Expressionist in design and conception, whenever lighting and/or a stylized stage design substitute for a more realistic one, then this will have occurred as a result of the director's innovations.[7] A careful look at O'Casey's texts, in both cases, reveals realistic stage settings which become luminous and symbolic only as the play itself unfolds. The kaleidoscopic transformations which do occur are carefully grounded in reality: in the red glare of the fire or in the miraculous colours of the sunset. Thus they are quite unlike the concluding vision of *A Dream Play*, for instance, where the flower bud that is the roof of the castle blossoms into a gigantic chrysanthemum (though O'Casey would later use somewhat similar effects for comedy). Such a transformation transcends reality altogether unless we wish to include, as Strindberg did, the 'reality' of our dreams.

The use of dreams and visions – often realized onstage with the aid of lighting effects and stylized, movable settings – is, of course, a very prominent characteristic of Expressionist drama. Their use is also the source of one of the most prevalent misconceptions concerning O'Casey's two visionary plays. Underlying almost every commentary on, and every production of, Act II of *The Tassie* and Act III of *Red Roses* is the implied or overt assumption that these two acts employ Strindberg's 'dream structure.' But, in *The Tassie*, if we do not focus exclusively on the effects of the stylized chanting and staccato speech and think, as well, in terms of character and action, there is only one scene – the obeisance to the gun (and even this scene does not defy the physical laws of the universe) – and nothing at all in Act III of *Red Roses* that cannot be understood within the framework of the waking world. If we described these acts as 'dreams' it must be understood that we are speaking metaphorically of visions, one diabolic and nightmarish, the other beatific, both of which are immanent in the natural world, and both of which can be revealed only to an awakened consciousness. As if to underline this difference, O'Casey has his characters actually drowse or sleep onstage and then awake to the reality of the vision they are experiencing.

While Strindberg's *A Dream Play* suggests the world itself to be an illusion or dream and thus demands throughout the concept of a dream structure which both his preface and title provide, O'Casey's visionary plays are often distorted, rather than illuminated, by this same concept. Such a concept is, in fact, antithetical to O'Casey's viewing of life and takes away from the strong sense of reality which so intensifies that moment of belief evoked by the vision before us. When these two acts are viewed purely as dream structures, however, the power which they should have is needlessly and wrongly dissipated. Rather than helping us to understand O'Casey's work, then, the label 'Expressionist,' with all its attendant definitions, frequently blurs and distorts, and, as we have seen, has even been used as a way of dismissing his work altogether.

On the other hand, the term 'expressionism' is obviously part of the critical vocabulary needed to explicate O'Casey's craftsmanship, especially in the area of the middle plays (from *The Tassie* to *Red Roses*). Though the fact that O'Casey himself (when questioned) objected to its use in relation to his plays suggests that he was aware of the damage that the term, used indiscriminately, had already done. In a letter to Vincent De Baun dated 17 April 1949, he replies in a mildly querulous vein (in a statement which is too often dismissed as simply having been spoken tongue-in-cheek): 'I've often heard of, & read about "naturalism" & "expressionism," but, God's truth, I don't know rightly what either means.'[8] Then, in a letter to Ronald G. Rollins dated 24 March 1960, O'Casey flatly denies that he 'consciously adopted expressionism, which I don't understand and never did.'[9] The change in tone can perhaps be construed as O'Casey's instinctive attempt to redress the balance in the face of a growing tendency to exaggerate both the extent and the nature of his commitment to continental Expressionism. For it is exactly this kind of exaggeration that has prevented our coming to grips with his experimental use of certain expressionist techniques as an integral part of his own realistic and symbolic structures.

Throughout his life, O'Casey was a fierce individualist, and he never forgave George Orwell for describing the style of *Drums under the Windows* as 'a sort of basic Joyce.'[10] As both the autobiographies and the articles make clear, O'Casey's dramatic craftsmanship does not depend on the theories of others, but rather upon the development of his own innate dramatic sense. For example, in 'The Plough and the Stars' in Retrospect,' O'Casey wrote: 'I never make a scenario, depending on the natural growth of a play rather than on any method of joinery' – a statement which material from the holographs confirms.[11] In his plays, then, it is only natural for him to change the techniques of continental Expressionism to suit his own specialized purposes: in the delineation of stage settings, in the portrayal of symbolic, elevated characters, in the use of choral groupings, and in the use of language. The startling and original effects which he achieves here can best be discerned when – rather than continuing to confuse O'Casey's 'homemade' expressionism with continental Expressionism – we compare, instead, those correspondences which do indeed exist between Toller's two earliest works, *Transfiguration* and *Masses and Man,* and O'Casey's two visionary plays, *The Silver Tassie* and *Red Roses for Me.*

8 Sean O'Casey's Bridge of Vision

ANTI-WAR PLAYS: 'MASSES AND MAN' AND
'THE SILVER TASSIE'

O'Casey's introduction to Expressionism came through the Dublin
Drama League's presentation of Toller's *Masses and Man* in 1922. Thus it
is not really surprising that this play should have come to the forefront of
O'Casey's mind when, some four years later, he began to write his own
anti-war play, *The Silver Tassie*, and, in the process, began to search
consciously for a new means of expression through new techniques.[12] In
Rose and Crown he writes:

There was no importance in trying to do the same thing again, letting the second
play imitate the first, and the third the second. He wanted a change from what the
Irish critics had called burlesque, photographic realism, or slices of life, though
the manner and method of two of the plays were as realistic as the scents stealing
from a gaudy bunch of blossoms.[13]

There has been much critical conjecture about what O'Casey meant by
this last statement, and it has frequently been used to spark the search for
expressionist techniques in his plays – and not without success. For
example, Joan Templeton writes: 'One finds the techniques of Expressionism in every full-length play from *The Plough and the Stars* in 1926 to
The Drums of Father Ned in 1958, and they figure significantly in the success
of the late comedies.'[14] Yet even with this renewed emphasis on
expressionist techniques throughout his work, it is difficult to recognize
O'Casey in Templeton's description of the second act of *The Tassie*, which
she thinks

qualifies as *thoroughly* Expressionist because it possesses the *dream structure*, a
deliberately distorted setting, exaggerated caricatures, and at its close, highly
symbolic stage action resembling pantomime and usually referred to by the term
'stylized.' It also has the special qualities of freneticism and grostesqueness found
in many of the German plays. The presence of a skeletal figure and the use of
many stage properties suggesting death are frequently found in German
Expressionism at the height of the movement when the 'graveyard scene' became
stock. Act II is an *Expressionist theme statement*: man may cling to the belief that he
worships a Christian God, but the real object of his worship is the power of wrath
and destruction.[15]

Certainly O'Casey was writing with the plays of the Expressionists in mind – the wheelchair as 'battle chariot,' for example, which Strindberg's cripple, Hummel, rides about in all day long 'like the god Thor himself,' careens madly out of the *The Ghost Sonata* and into the last two acts of *The Silver Tassie*. However, affinities in theme, or even of image, character, or situation, do not necessarily lead to the use of the 'same' techniques or the same dream-like effects.

For instance, what would O'Casey have thought of Toller's 'Letter to a Creative Producer,' which appeared as the foreword to the second German edition of *Masses and Man* in 1922? There, Toller agrees with his producer's decision to give the three 'realistic' scenes a 'dream-like' or 'visionary' air, with the resultant blurring of the boundary between dream and reality. In production, the workman's tavern of the first scene, with its whitewashed walls and pictures of proletarian heroes, had been replaced by a platform with steps leading down into a 'seething' darkness, the characters being illuminated by three shafts of light. 'What can be realistic in my drama "Man and the Masses"?' Toller asks. 'Only the spiritual, the intellectual qualities.'[16] This kind of abstraction – and much of the play consists of abstractions mouthed by cardboard characters – would be anathema to O'Casey's artistic vision.

'Your strong point is characterisation,'[17] Lady Gregory had told O'Casey when he first submitted manuscripts to the Abbey Theatre and, though he grew tired of being reminded of it by others, he was not about to forget this valuable piece of advice. Unlike Toller, O'Casey did not leave realistic characters and stage settings behind in his excursion into expressionism.

Thus, in Act II of *The Tassie*, despite the nightmarish quality inherent largely in the terrifying ritual which is about to unfold, O'Casey begins, as always, with a scene of minutely detailed realism:

> *In the war zone: a scene of jagged and lacerated ruin of what was once a monastery. At back a lost wall and window are indicated by an arched piece of broken coping pointing from the left to the right, and a similar piece of masonry pointing from the right to the left. Between these two lacerated fingers of stone can be seen the country stretching to the horizon where the front trenches are.* (p 35)

Of this scene, Raymond Massey, the first director of *The Silver Tassie*, notes in his autobiography: 'O'Casey's delineation of the setting, running to more than a page of script, went far beyond the brief indications usually made by playwrights.' And when Augustus John read it he immediately 'went to a cabinet ... and took out some large charcoal drawings which he said were part of the collection of sketches he had made at the war front for the Canadian government ... Most of the drawings ... were of ruins, shell holes, wrecked equipment, wire, mud, desolation and destruction.' The sketch he chose as being remarkably like O'Casey's setting had 'the ruined wall of a chapel with the window at the right and a broken archway to the left.'[18] Expressionist act or not, the scene was one Augustus John had observed and documented many times at the front. In fact, this particular choice of setting – the ruins of a monastery in wartime – adequately explains on a perfectly realistic basis many elements of the scene which are usually thought of as purely Expressionist: for example, the life-size crucifix, the chanting of the monks, the gigantic howitzer gun, and the ruins of the houses with 'lean, dead hands ... protruding' (p 35).

Even the most absurd and grotesque elements, such as the wooden signs, 'Hyde Park Corner' and 'No Hawkers or Street Crie[r]s Permitted Here' (one at the base of the gun, the other at the entrance to the Red Cross Station), which seem at first to have only the kind of disjointed effect that we encounter in dreams, are realized, upon reflection, to be exactly the right touch of reality to give to the scene. This is just the kind of practical joke that soldiers who are having a moment's respite from the trenches will engage in to raise their flagging spirits. But to translate this setting, which is so strongly rooted in reality, into a bronze and silver extravaganza complete with skeletons hanging from the barbed wire, as was done in the 1972 Abbey production, is to move very far away from O'Casey's stated intention of a scene only 'a *little* distorted from its original appearance' (p 36, italics mine).

Just how far O'Casey was willing to go in his mingling of realism and expressionism can easily be discerned by comparing the description of the Croucher in the 1928 version of the text (the one used by Massey in the 1929 Apollo production in London) with the description in the Stage Version of *The Tassie*, published by Macmillan in 1949. The early version is clearly realistic, for O'Casey writes: 'Crouching near the fire is a soldier whose clothes are covered with mud and splashed with blood.'[19] The description in the later text, however, not only incorporates Massey's elevation of the Croucher on a ramp overlooking the other soldiers (an innovation which, as shown in the following chapter, has far-reaching implications), but also, in other ways, moves the figure closer to continental Expressionism, particularly to Ernst Toller's skeleton-like creations. O'Casey's 'Notes' which preface the Stage Version specify that *the Croucher's make-up should come as close as possible to a death's head, a skull; and his hands should show like those of a skeleton's. He should sit somewhere above the group of Soldiers; preferably to one side, on the left, from view-point of audience, so as to overlook the Soldiers. He should look languid, as if very tired of life.* (p 3)

But, unlike Toller's creations, which O'Casey later criticized as being 'too much skeletonized; not enough of the plumpness of life,'[20] the Croucher maintains his humanity. For what O'Casey records in the haunting face of this despairing soldier is a phenomenon which can be observed in the very sick or the very old when the skin takes on a transparent quality and the skeleton structure beneath becomes almost visible. The soldier has given up the struggle for life, and when he speaks it is to intone a prophecy of doom:

And I prophesied, and the breath came out of them, and the sinews came away from them, and behold a shaking, and their bones fell asunder, bone from his bone, and they died, and the exceeding great army became a valley of dry bones. (pp. 36–7)

The result is electrifying, partly because his denial of the life-giving prophecy of Ezekiel is validated by the stark realism of the desolate scene before us, partly because, in the context of the Kyrie Eleison intoned by an unseen figure in the ruined monastery, the Croucher's words have the effect of a Black Mass.[21]

Yet essentially the biblical chant is no different in kind from Susie's prophetic chanting at the beginning of the realistic first act: 'Man walketh in a vain shadow, and disquieteth himself in vain: He heapeth up riches, and cannot tell who shall gather them' (p 7). Nor is it entirely unlike the eerie prophesying of Bessie in *The Plough and the Stars*, though there her natural idiom of speech breaks through the biblical language to keep it firmly anchored in reality. Thus, when the curtain opens on Act II of *The Silver Tassie*, what the audience should see initially is a scene which has much more in common with what has gone before in O'Casey's own work and much less in common with the work of the Expressionists than has ordinarily been supposed. If, on the contrary, what the audience sees is a 'thoroughly Expressionist' act – complete with 'rotting skeletons'[22] – then it is because the director and stage designer have exaggerated what they understood to be the Expressionist qualities of the scene and ignored the very strong element of realism which is present. Though the implied symbolism of the setting, as the ritual of the mass is enacted, becomes increasingly apparent, the effect should be perfectly in keeping with O'Casey's own particular kind of heightened realism.

Such characteristically detailed stage directions as those in Act II of *The Tassie* show that O'Casey demanded clarity of outline in the construction of his plays, and the impact so gained is achieved precisely because the scene, for all its grotesque quality, retains, at the same time, a grimly realistic air. Any uncalled-for distortion or blurring of outline, any exaggeration of the Expressionist elements of the stage setting, as was done in the 1972 revival at the Abbey, would not only lessen the impact of the play as a whole, but would also destroy its unity. The reviewer who wrote of this production that he would like to see Act II produced 'as a piece on its own, since it clearly would stand alone quite divorced from the tragedy of Harry Heegan,' and that he doubted whether any director could ever make the end of the play 'work,'[23] confirms a growing conviction that the success of the second act of *The Silver Tassie* continues to be bought at the expense of the last two acts: O'Casey's debt to Expressionism is inadvertently being used to bankrupt his play.

If, on the other hand, Act II of *The Tassie* is to be seen as an organic part of the play – a problem Raymond Massey grappled with in the Apollo production[24] – then it needs to be understood as much more than a horrifying glimpse of the nightmare into which the participants of war are plunged. It should be understood and realized onstage not simply as a symbolic dream structure, or an 'Expressionist theme statement,' but as a narrative episode essential to the development of the entire play. As such, Act II shows the soldiers' participation in a diabolic ritual: a Black Mass in which we witness nothing less than the invocation – and descent – of the God of War, and his incarnation in man. This haunting portrait of man possessed by the spirit of war is presented ironically in Act I; demonically in Act II; both realistically and symbolically in Acts III and IV.

The concrete portrayal of such an experience is part of what gives the play its awesome magnitude and, ultimately, gives a sense of psychological reality to characters who otherwise may appear two-dimensional and unconvincing. For this reason Act II is essential to the credibility of the play and its characters, a credibility which is achieved, almost paradoxically, by enlarging the scope of the action and magnifying the dimensions of the characters by the employment of techniques which are usually thought of as 'Expressionist.' And so with the entrance of the anonymous soldiers who have just come from twelve weary hours of transport fatigue, and who speak in chorus as they complain of being 'cold and wet and tir'd' (p 37), the act departs even more noticeably from what we have been taught to think of as the 'uncompromising' realism of O'Casey's 'early' manner.

Initially, the soldiers may seem to be a group caricature in the manner, say, of the guards in Toller's *Masses and Man*. There, in the fourth 'Dream Picture,' the guards are not in any way individualized but are interlocked by the regularly rhyming stanzas and the repetition of the hummed chorus into a symbolic figure who embodies one of the main causes of the revolution. O'Casey's soldiers, on the other hand, are interlocked physically as well as by the choral effect of their speech. Yet their stylized entrance (devised originally by Massey, but incorporated by O'Casey into the Stage Version) has a realistic basis in the exhaustion of the soldiers: '[they] should enter in a close mass, as if each was keeping the other from falling, utterly weary and tired out. They should appear as if they were almost locked together' (p 3). Similarly, the stylized, chanted dialogue – as it grows slower and more dream-like – serves, on the realistic plane, to add to our sense of the soldiers' weariness.

At the same time, it is clear that O'Casey is taking pains to ground the language in reality by using the Cockney idiom, which contrasts strangely with the sonorous biblical language of the Croucher and the intoning of the Latin Mass. Though the predominant acccent is that of the Cockney, the Dublin accent of the 4th Soldier – the one who looks 'very like Teddy' (p 37) – should also at times be distinguished. But it is the 1st Soldier who plays the largest part: he recalls 'the missus paryding along Walham Green' and imagines his daugher Emmie asking for a balloon only to be told she cannot have one until her father's "ome, an' the bands a-plying!' (p 38). More than anything else, it is this sympathetic family portrait that makes the scene real in a way which is uniquely O'Casey's own, and reveals the 1st Soldier – like the 4th – to be more than a symbolic figure in a caricatured sketch of soldiers at war.

In other words, whenever O'Casey employs stylized or symbolic characters, he is careful to prevent them from dwindling away into two- (or even one-) dimensional figures – unless occasionally, as with Foster and Dowzard in *Red Roses*, he deliberately intends this kind of dehumanizing effect. If his symbolic characters do not actually grow in stature (as is the case with the Croucher, who achieves that mysterious fourth dimension which is 'soul' or 'spirit'), they at least retain enough breadth and depth to appear, as one reviewer aptly puts it, 'alive with a strong life.'[25]

The Visitor is a good example of this type of character building, since his telegraphic style of communication, while reminiscent of Wedekind, is employed by O'Casey in a way which blends expressionism and realism. Not only do the Visitor's staccato phrases link him, first, to the Corporal, and, finally, to the Croucher, as an indication of the mechanized and rote-like nature of their momentary 'spiritual' kinship, but the total effect is also strangely realistic. For the terse phrases impart an air of urgency to the scene as they cut through the pervading atmosphere of weariness conveyed by the soldiers' chants. It is this sense of urgency the Visitor feels which adds to his air of self-importance as he revels in the experience of war, all the while being careful to avoid any areas of real danger. Thus, a miniature Miles Gloriosus springs to life as O'Casey turns caricature into character at a touch. Moreover, when the Corporal's earthy reference to 'the arses of the guns' (p 40) embarrasses the Visitor and renders him, for the moment, almost speechless, the dimensions which are added again prevent that sense of a two-dimensional cardboard figure so frequently associated with Expressionist theatre.

AUTOBIOGRAPHICAL PLAYS: 'TRANSFIGURATION' AND 'RED ROSES FOR ME'

While in his later writings O'Casey grew more critical of Toller's work and of Expressionism in general, he always admired that wildly imaginative quality – the dancing skeletons, the fox-trotting bankers in top-hats – that would not be bound by the limits of the realistic stage. Then, too, O'Casey must have sympathized with Toller's youthful idealism and the personal courage with which he acted throughout his life.

In life, as in his plays, Toller was a spokesman for the masses in a machine-ridden society and cried out indignantly against the abuses of power and wealth which he considered characteristic of the bourgeoisie. Though, like Friedrich in *Transfiguration,* Toller fought in the German army during the early years of World War I, he afterwards helped to organize labour strikes as a way of stopping the war. He played an active role in the Bavarian Revolution of 1918, but was imprisoned when the revolution was suppressed. In prison, Toller completed *Transfiguration* (1918) and then went on to write *Masses and Man* (1921). Despite their loose and unintegrated structure, which seems to be partly the result of experimental methods of craftsmanship, these early plays of Toller are considerable achievements for a writer then only in his mid-twenties and proved to be well worth O'Casey's admiring attention.[26]

Red Roses for Me, in particular, contains situations and themes so similar to Toller's *Transfiguration* that the latter might be thought of as the 'source' of the O'Casey play, as well as being – together with *Masses and Man* – the source of O'Casey's anti-war play, *The Silver Tassie*. As in *Red Roses for Me*, there is the ardent young artist and humanitarian who feels himself to have been betrayed by the girl he loves, and who turns to help the revolutionary cause of labour. As in *The Silver Tassie*, there is the young man in the prime of life, fighting in a war which is recognized to be a senseless nightmare of horror. Friedrich, like Harry Heegan, is wounded, and the hospital scenes in both plays (as well as the war zone scenes) show the total disillusionment of the 'heroes' as they see themselves and their comrades victimized by inhuman states and institutions. Friedrich's smashing of the war memorial he is sculpting is not unlike Harry's crushing of the silver tassie, for both have become symbols of a victory which is empty and bitter. And Act III of *Red Roses* – O'Casey's 'transfiguration' scene – corresponds to the concluding scene of the Toller play, though Friedrich's transformation as shown in the 'dream' scenes has no exact parallel in the O'Casey play. Finally, in a way which is typical of much Expressionist writing,[27] both dramatists make use of Christian symbolism and ritual in order to portray Christ-like figures who take upon themselves the sufferings of the world.

However, while these similarities illustrate O'Casey's continuing fascination with the experiments of such Expressionists as Toller, he also realized, for example, that it is not enough to make an appointment for noon the next day in the marketplace in order to talk about transfiguration. Instead, so that Ayamonn may actually reveal the ever-present possibility of a world redeemed, the colours and images realized in the lyricism of his poetry are simultaneously made concrete onstage by appropriate effects of lighting, setting, and costuming. Thus Ayamonn's words have the magical effect of creating the transformed world we see before us. And in this world – miraculously – we catch a glimpse, not only of Dublin as a truly Irish madonna, a Kathleen ni Houlihan who is both beautiful and true, but also of the legendary heroes of Ireland's Celtic past, whose spirit is reborn in the men and women that Ayamonn will lead into battle. Here, as in Act II of *The Tassie*, O'Casey makes plain that the ideal, like the demonic, exists within the actual – hidden, yet always waiting to be revealed.

To compare O'Casey's transfiguration scene,[28] with Toller's, then, is to become aware that O'Casey, while influenced by Toller's work and capitalizing on his daring innovations, has been able to combine expressionism and realism in a dramatically effective way, whereas Toller, in his dependence upon a 'creative Producer' to achieve this kind of unifying effect, has clearly reached the limits of his craft. Ironically, the transfiguration scene which ends the Toller play is not designated as being 'on the borderline between reality and unreality,'[29] though it desperately needs an Expressionist context to create the aura of a dream scene in which the psychologically unmotivated actions of the characters will appear more acceptable:

> FRIEDRICH You are all of you, all of you, no longer men and women; you are distorted images of your real selves.
>
> And yet you could still be men and women, still be human, if only you had faith in yourselves and in humanity, if only you would grant the spirit its fulfilment ...
>
> Oh, if only you were men and women – men and women unqualified – free men and women!
>
> (*During this long speech there has been ever-increasing disturbance among the crowd. Some have kneeled down. Others, weeping, bury their heads in their hands. Some lie broken on the ground. These now rise again in gladness; others open wide their arms to heaven...*)
>
> ALL We are men and women! (*Softly, as though smiling to themselves.*) We are men and women! (p 105)

Far from being men and women, Toller's characters remain cardboard figures who fail to spring to life as O'Casey's characters seldom fail to do. There are several reasons for this failure, not the least of which is Toller's willingness (as we have seen) to forego the illusion of reality, including the psychological reality which makes the actions of the characters believable, no matter how odd or unusual these actions themselves may be. O'Casey, on the other hand, realized instinctively in his plays what, in later years, he set down clearly in one of his essays: 'However high and lofty this moral life may be, even allowing that it is beyond the searching mind of man, it is useless, and can do nix without the help and presence of the despised body.'[30] To depict the 'moral life' as a spiritual reality only, as Toller tried to do, results, finally, in a failure to depict anything living at all.

THE STOCK GRAVEYARD SCENE

The validity of this statement becomes even more apparent when we compare the effects achieved by the 'graveyard' scene in *The Silver Tassie* with those achieved in the corresponding scenes of *Transfiguration.* Toller juxtaposes the dream-like 'No-Man's Land' with the realism of the immediately preceding war zone scene in a way which clearly intends the one to reinforce and intensify the mood of the other. Though O'Casey must have assimilated from Toller the technique of juxtaposing expressionism and realism within the same play, O'Casey develops the technique to a point where he is able to mingle the two methods within individual scenes and acts to create an effect which is all the more powerful because it is immediate and 'real.' By contrast, the effect Toller wishes to create is not intensified, but dissipated, as the spectacle of the talking, laughing, dancing skeletons finally loses all credibility.

So long as the skeletons discuss the isolation, the cold, the pain and suffering which war brings, so long as the focus is upon the dismembered bodies and the pitifully transient fame which they have sought, the scene at least maintains the appropriate note of macabre horror and a strong sense of the futility and absurdity of war:

> The coloured ribbons on our chests
> Have long ago decayed.
> Our names were in the newspapers
> All bordered round with black. (p 71)

However, when Toller wishes to reach the highest pitch of emotional intensity, to create an effect which is meant to be overwhelming, the scene instead becomes ineffective. The spectacle of skeletons covering their 'nakedness' with their hands as a thirteen-year-old girl skeleton is suddenly discovered in their midst is merely silly. Nor can the dialogue support the metaphor of war as 'rapacious' in terms of the sexual violation of an innocent victim, a child, when that child is depicted as a skeleton who must first identify herself and then relate what has happened:

> SKELETON (*half-hidden*) ...
> Even to-day I don't know why they did it.
> Did it really have to be like that, sir?
> One had hardly gone away
> Before the next got into bed with me.
> SECOND SKELETON And then?
> SKELETON (*half-hidden*) And then ... I died of it. (p 72)

Here, the mood which Toller is creating threatens, by its very shrillness, to run completely out of control. The 'grotesque that does not cause laughter'[31] may unintentionally cause laughter and so lose the effect of horror and dread which the dramatist is trying to achieve. Although we may read with a certain intellectual curiosity, the scene (unlike the gravedigger's scene in *Hamlet*) does not demand our emotional involvement, for it is continually interrupted by passages which fail to provide any touchstone of reality and hence cannot but fail to sustain the appropriate emotional response.

In *The Tassie*, however, 'the criss-cross pattern of the barbed wire bordering the trenches' (p 35) is certainly more effective without the skeletons caught on the wire that Toller provides, especially when we recall from Act I the ironic context in which Harry Heegan introduces the song 'The Silver Tassie': 'The song that the little Jock used to sing, Barney, what was it? The little Jock we left shrivellin' on the wire after the last push' (p 27). The memory of Harry's cruel words is evoked by the barbed wire illuminated in the red glare from the brazier, the dead hands (not, strictly speaking, skeleton hands) stretching upward from the rubble, the suggestion of a death's head in the appearance of the Croucher, the grotesque figure of the 'crucified' Barney, and the ritualized chanting of the Black Mass. All of these are more effective, as they are more tightly concentrated and controlled, than are Toller's numerous perambulating, talking, and dancing skeletons. Far from creating a 'stock' graveyard scene, O'Casey has daringly rejuvenated what had become, at the hands of the Expressionists, a telltale sign of the decadence of their art. As he does so often, O'Casey has out-expressioned the Expressionists in a way which, as shown in the concluding chapter, has clearly anticipated some of the more daring effects of the Theatre of the Absurd.

DANCES OF LIFE AND DEATH

The differences in technique between Toller's work and O'Casey's result naturally enough from a basically different concept of character, a concept clearly reflected in their own lives. Thus, Toller's characters often exist simply as mouthpieces for their author's ideas, whereas O'Casey's characters, whatever their symbolic dimensions, continue to live in their own right.

Even in *The Tassie*, where Harry Heegan's individual identity 'dissolves' into the largely symbolic figure of the Croucher and the anonymous soldiers of the second act, it is only through the complex interrelationship of the Croucher with Harry Heegan that we realize the depth and universality of O'Casey's vision and of the characters he has created. For not only does the demonic portrait of the Croucher reveal the incarnation of the spirit of war in man, but, in so doing, it also reveals the kind of experience which has collided with Harry Heegan, and with many others, in such a way as to change, irreversibly, the patterns of their lives. The experience is larger than any one individual; it is dominant, powerful, unavoidable; it is man's fate, the antagonist with which he wrestles or under whose thumb he is crushed. And yet O'Casey returns to the more realistic portrayal of individuals in the third and fourth acts of the play, as he continues to show us the sometimes tragic, sometimes comic, workings out of destiny in the lives of individual men.

In *Masses and Man*, on the other hand, Toller's 'characters' remain little more than symbols of much larger forces, for Toller believed, as W.H. Auden recognized, that 'We are lived by powers we pretend to understand.'[32] Ironically, even his central figure, Sonia, becomes abstracted as the symbol of the Individual, though she is modelled on a real person and one Toller greatly admired.[33] In *Transfiguration* only Friedrich struggles part way to life as a thinly disguised symbol of the socially committed Artist – Toller himself. In fact, as these two works suggest, Toller must have at times felt himself to be an insignificant part of forces running out of control. His attempts to shape political events, like O'Casey's less ambitious attempts, were to fail; and, unable to regain control, as O'Casey did, by placing his political ideals in the service of his art, Toller was finally crushed by these forces – forces that burned his books, that made him flee the beginning of the Nazi 'holocaust,' and that finally led him to take his own life. In retrospect, the artistic failure of Toller's transfiguration scene serves as a prelude to these larger catastrophes, and the skeletons' dance of death as a foreshadowing of the event that was to end his own life so tragically.[34]

O'Casey's own life, by contrast, is the embodiment of an energy skilfully controlled and intelligently directed, pitted successfully against forces much larger than himself: the poverty and filth of the Dublin slums; the near-blindness which shadowed his childhood and prevented him from learning to read until he was fourteen; the political fortunes and misfortunes of Ireland; the two world wars; the death of his son, Niall; and the *Silver Tassie* controversy, which confirmed his self-exile and which continued to threaten his work as a dramatist. O'Casey's plays reflect his incredible vitality, the irresistible life force symbolized by the cock in *Cock-a-Doodle Dandy*, and his characters, like their creator, are fiercely individualistic. In a memorial article written shortly after

O'Casey's death, David Krause relates an anecdote which really says the most important thing there is to say about O'Casey's 'philosophy' of life. In the midst of a serious conversation about his life and work, O'Casey suddenly got up

and enacted an energetic mime-dance, pacing around the room in an exaggerated strut, raising himself on tip-toe with each swinging stride and flapping his arms so that he looked like a comical old bird trying to fly and not quite making it. 'It keeps me from forgetting,' [he explained,] 'that human beings are gay and funny fellas.'[35]

This unquenchable gaiety is what allows O'Casey to view life, not as tragedy, but as tragi-comedy. And his ability to laugh in the face of misfortune is what – more often than not – rescues his work from the overt didacticism so characteristic of Toller.

In thus recognizing the most fundamental differences between the two men – both in their lives and in their art – we can better understand the nature of O'Casey's debt to Ernst Toller – the acknowledgement of which would go a long way towards clarifying O'Casey's indebtedness to the Expressionist movement as a whole. Moreover, once O'Casey's use of expressionism is recognized and understood, then the stylistic unity of his work, from early plays to late, can also be discerned. Perhaps more importantly, the organic unity of the individual plays can be reassessed. For example, far from being disunified by their curious mingling of styles, *The Silver Tassie* and *Red Roses for Me* juxtapose and blend realism and expressionism in a way which allows O'Casey to achieve a new kind of unity – one in which he is able to achieve effects which go far beyond the limitations of each technique used individually. In fact, as they define their own organic form and create their own principles of unity, these two visionary plays best illustrate the kind of realistic and symbolic structures that O'Casey, throughout his life, delighted in building.

2

The Silver Tassie

Two years after receiving the Hawthornden Prize for *Juno and the Paycock* – an event which closely followed the riots over *The Plough* (1926) – Sean O'Casey made literary history in a quite different fashion by quarrelling with the Abbey directorate over the rejection of his first clearly experimental play, *The Silver Tassie*. W.B. Yeats, as the most prominent director of the Abbey Theatre, was largely responsible for the play's rejection, and though he allowed *The Tassie* to be performed at the Abbey in 1935, he never really changed his mind about the play. But it was O'Casey, himself, who chose to turn the rejection, of what he obviously thought to be his masterpiece, into a public scandal. Indeed, in later years, he seemed to recognize a certain inevitability about what had occurred, for, as he commented in a letter to his American agent, 'I've never written anything that didn't cause a dispute, a row, a difference, or something.'[1] O'Casey loved 'mental fight,' just as surely as he hated 'corporeal' war, and, in retrospect, the *Silver Tassie* controversy (as well as all the smaller controversies surrounding the later plays) can be seen, in part, as a reflection of his own pugnacious spirit. Yet now, since the celebration of the centenary of his birth, perhaps the time has come for the caricatured figure of O'Casey the fighting Irishman – the one his detractors still hasten to attack – to pass into history, so that it can be replaced by the more complete portrait of the man that is reflected by the larger body of his works.

Though O'Casey was not, as he believed, the victim of an Abbey directorate conspiracy, he was, and still is, the victim of 'Yeatsean arrogance,' of what O'Casey himself mockingly called 'the conceit of

Zeusian infallibility.'² 'Solving' the *Silver Tassie* controversy, then, means breaking free of this conceit altogether by appealing, not so much to external sources, as to the play itself. Let *The Tassie* – both the texts and the productions – resolve the only really serious charge brought against the play by Yeats: the charge that *The Tassie* is disunified both stylistically and in terms of character and action. Here we will find that, in keeping with the tradition of experimental theatre, a more innovative approach is needed: one that, startling as it may seem at first, would nevertheless allow for the possibility of *The Silver Tassie* being realized more successfully onstage.

In replying to Yeats' long letter which attempted to explain why the Abbey had rejected the play, O'Casey lampoons all Yeats' talk of unities, saying: 'I have held these infants in my arms a thousand times and they are all the same – fat, lifeless, wrinkled things that give one a pain in his belly looking at them.'³ The reply is vintage O'Casey: anger and pain transmuted magically by wit. But O'Casey does more than mock Yeats; he suggests a way of answering him:

I'm afraid I can't make my mind mix with the sense of importance you give to 'a dominating character.' God forgive me, but it does sound as if you peeked and pined for a hero in the play. Now, is a dominating character more important than a play, or is a play more important than a dominating character? You say that 'my power in the past has been the creation of a unique character that dominated all round him, and was a main impulse in some action that filled the play from beginning to end.' In 'The Silver Tassie' you have a unique work that dominates all the characters in the play.⁴

At first, in his haste to contradict Yeats, O'Casey seems to be implying that there is no dominating character in *The Tassie*, a statement which is clearly not true. For Harry Heegan dominates three acts of the play and the Croucher dominates Act II. The final statement is clear enough, however, since it suggests that all the characters in the play are dominated, and therefore, in a sense unified, by the central theme – or 'character' – of the play itself. And the central theme of *The Tassie* is war: war possesses all the characters in the play and dominates them. The relationship, then, between Act II and the rest of the play, both symbolically and in terms of character and action, is bound up in the mystery of an individual identity – Harry Heegan's – caught up, overshadowed, and possessed by the dark forces of war. The unravelling of this mystery involves our understanding of the complex sense in which Harry Heegan is, paradoxically, both a man crucified by war and, at the same time, an embodiment of the spirit of war: both a Christ and an anti-Christ. In the strange figure of the Croucher, as will be demonstrated, all these identities merge, so that, as both character and symbol – of a power much larger than himself – Harry Heegan becomes the dominating force *throughout* the play.

O'Casey must have been greatly distressed to find that Yeats was unable to realize anything of the magnitude of *The Tassie*'s vision. Worse still, Yeats had accused him of knowing nothing of his subject: 'You are not interested in the Great War; you never stood on its battlefields or walked its hospitals, and so write out of your opinions.'[5] But it was the well-meant suggestion that the Abbey's rejection of *The Tassie* be kept secret that angered O'Casey to the point where he did himself the irrevocable disservice of making the rejection and Yeats' damning criticisms of *The Tassie* public.

Thus, despite the fact that Raymond Massey's brilliant direction of *The Silver Tassie* at the Apollo Theatre in October 1929 went further towards unifying the play onstage than any subsequent production has yet done, reviewers and critics have never had the opportunity of seeing the play except in the context of Yeats' critical remarks, a context which has contributed immeasurably to the difficulty of viewing the play – so far ahead of its time in style and technique – as anything other than a disunified structure, though its inexplicably gripping power has come to be almost universally recognized. Not so surprisingly, then, even other-wise favourable reviews of the Apollo production echoed Yeats' criticism: 'It lacks the homogeneity, the essential unity of a really good play,'[6] wrote the critic for *The New Statesman* in the 19 October 1929 edition.

Moreover, in calling the play 'too abstract'[7] Yeats had prepared the way for the more specific charge of 'Expressionism,' 'that word, that method, that mistake!'[8] levelled against the same production by Richard Jennings of *The Spectator*, and for the growing conviction that the play, with its strange mixture of expressionism and realism, is also irrevocably dis-unified stylistically. The play ran for only twenty-six performances at the Apollo, though Massey tells us in his autobiography, *A Hundred Different Lives*, that C.B. Cochran, the producer, thought of *The Tassie* as his 'proudest failure.'[9] To complete the paradox, the expressionism of the play, in 1929, could not help but discredit it at the box office, whereas today – such are the vagaries even of literary fashion – it is frequently the expressionism of the second act that helps to draw the audience. And with each relatively more successful revival, there has actually been an added incentive to increase the stylistic disunity of the play by exaggerating the expressionism of Act II out of all proportion to O'Casey's original intention.

There were other critics, too, who agreed with Jennings that 'we must not be too hard upon the Abbey Theatre. It had a case.'[10] And their frequent use of the term 'caricature' seems to confirm what had been Walter Starkie's opinion of the play: 'In *The Silver Tassie* the characters seem to come from a shadow world; they are not beings of flesh and blood ... He was not able to create, as he did before, living men and women.'[11] Oddly, though he disliked *The Tassie*, Starkie was the one director who clearly asserted O'Casey's right to have the Abbey produce the play. But Lennox Robinson was adamant in his refusal. 'It is a bad play,'[12] he told Lady Gregory categorically. His words are echoed, yet strangely qualified, some forty years later, by Hugh Leonard writing in *Plays and Players* of the Aldwych's revival: 'It is [a] bad, a terrible play. Perversely, but not incompatibly, it is also a masterpiece.'[13]

'It's All Very Curious, Isn't It?' – the title of an article which appears in *The Flying Wasp* – is O'Casey's 'reply' to criticism of this sort. How can *The Tassie* be 'a terrible play' and also 'a masterpiece'? O'Casey had ample time throughout his more than forty years as a creative artist to grow tired of the 'flawed genius' label. And nowhere is it more in evidence than in the *Silver Tassie* controversy, the place where it all began.

THE WINNING OF THE GRAIL

At present, however, the theatrical history of *The Silver Tassie*, beginning with the Apollo production, reflects not only this continuing controversy but also a fascination with certain aspects of the play, both structural and thematic. In fact, as reviewers and critics have so often noted, *The Tassie* may well be called a 'passion play.' For the element of ritual which the term suggests is readily confirmed, not just in the expressionism of Act II, but in the play as a whole. As well as the protagonist, Harry Heegan, certain other characters – Sylvester Heegan and Simon Norton, for example – have, from the beginning of the play, a symbolic as well as a realistic role. These two characters, who bear a generic resemblance to Boyle and Joxer, are the comic, music hall duo who appear at the opening curtain and slapstick their way mindlessly through what is undoubtedly O'Casey's most savage and bitter play. Yet, at moments, they also appear as stylized as figures in a Greek chorus.

The strongly ritualistic basis on which O'Casey builds – clearly underlined in the Apollo production by Massey's innovative use of elevations and doubling – was first articulated by Winifred Smith in her article 'The Dying God in the Modern Theatre.' She writes:

The opening act, as Shaw observed, is far from realistic, though a first glance at the stage shows a recognizable Irish [tenement] room, whose homely life is centered around the hearth; a second glance is more revealing, for it falls on the object in the middle of the room, a table covered with a purple cloth, like an altar, on which are displayed various gold and silver medals won by Harry; behind it a window opens toward the sea, showing a mast in the form of a cross, with a starry light at its top. Susie, quoting Scripture – an Old Testament prophecy of doom – as she polishes Harry's arms, is obviously the priestess serving the altar; just as obviously the two old men by the fire, in their reminiscences of the young hero's prowess, are the chorus celebrating the divine superiority of the chosen youth. These three prepare [for] the entrance of Harry, who is at last borne into the room on the shoulders of a Bacchanalian crowd, the girls with 'their skirts kilted above their knees' in true Maenad fashion; he and his sweetheart, Jessie, drink from the Silver Tassie, the Grail, the cup of communion, that will soon be full of his blood as it is now full of the wine of rejoicing.[14]

O'Casey, himself, in a letter to Ronald G. Rollins, confirms that much of the play's symbolic design is a conscious one:

Yes, *The Silver Tassie* is concerned with the futile sacrifice of a young hero in war, and the symbols, the chanted poetry and the ritual of sacrifice are embedded in the drama ... I wanted a war play without noise, without the interruptions of gunfire, content to show its results, as in the chant of the wounded and in the maiming of Harry; to show it in *its main spiritual phases*, its inner impulses and its actual horror of destroying the golden bodies of the young, and of the Church's damned approval in the sardonic hymn to the gun in Act II.[15]

O'Casey's letter shows, too, that his intent is satiric, that the ritual of human sacrifice as enacted in the war and approved by the Church is a barbaric thing. The play questions, not only the purpose of war, but also the purpose of those rituals, age-old and time-immemorial, which seek to give a meaning to the sacrifices of the golden bodies of the young that war demands. It is not that the ritual, in itself, is wrong, but that it has been used wrongly. Thus, in Act II, the ritual of the mass becomes a Black Mass, a way of condoning death, not when it is an inevitable part of a natural cycle, but when it is the conscious choice of a state and a church dedicated to war for reasons which, if not allowed to remain obscure, turn out, finally, to be perverse. O'Casey does not speak specifically of the Great War, however, for *The Silver Tassie*, as thesis play, probes the issues involved, not on any narrowly partisan level, but on a much more universal one.

Yet the play grew out of an intensely personal experience, as O'Casey tried to explain in his letter to Yeats. 'And does war consist only of battlefields?' he asks pointedly; then, after talking about the autobiographical element in *The Tassie*, he concludes by asking the question a second time:

But I have walked some of the hospital wards. I have talked and walked and smoked and sung with the blue-suited wounded men fresh from the front. I've been with the armless, the legless, the blind, the gassed, and the shell-shocked; one with a head bored by shrapnel ... with one whose head rocked like a frantic moving pendulum. Did you know 'Pantosser,' and did you ever speak to him? ... Or did you know Barney Fay, who got field punishment No. 1 for stealin' poultry (an Estaminay cock, maybe) behind the trenches, in the rest camps, out in France? And does war consist only of hospital wards and battlefields?[16]

As this passage clearly shows, the painful awareness summed up in *The Tassie* by Harry's bitter words, 'the Lord hath given and man hath taken away!' (p 102), springs from an overwhelming sense of pity for, and sympathy with, the wounded soldiers O'Casey had actually known. Here is the antithesis of the oversimplified and basically callous attitude towards the victims of war – such as Harry – expressed in the words of the song:

For he is a life on the ebb,
We a full life on the flow! (p 103)

In *The Tassie*, then, O'Casey shows that a society too willingly committing itself to war is composed of individuals whose unthinking and selfish attitudes permit the sacrifice of sons, husbands, and lovers in warfare. The artificial flowers so carefully arranged in the symbolic setting of Act I are a sure sign that there is no longer the reverence for life which we find in the women of the Dublin trilogy, and, later, in Ayamonn's mother in *Red Roses for Me*. It is not a pretty picture O'Casey is painting, and critics have been quick to point out the 'gallery of predatory women,'[17] so unlike Juno and Mary Boyle, and Nora Clitheroe. The fact is, to recognize at last the implications of O'Casey's deliberately rhetorical question, war 'consists' of much more than hospital wards and battlefields.

A warlike spirit resides in the attitudes of men and women who are habitually in a state of war with one another.

Thus, while the legend of Harry Heegan's exploits on the playing field and the 'chronicle' of how he stretched the Bobby 'hors dee combaa' (p 9) on the ground make such mock wars seem laughable enough, comedy begins to modulate towards tragedy when Teddy Foran returns from the trenches without having learned anything about 'the sacredness of life' (p 20). Mrs Foran's tearful description of her china being strewn about like 'flotsum an' jetsum' (p 34), a memorable colloquialism which she uses again in the hospital scene to refer to the wounded soldiers, points to the parallel O'Casey is drawing. Similarly, Teddy's smashing of the wedding bowl prepares for Harry's crushing of the silver tassie later in the play, for both actions symbolize a broken communion. This use of quarrels and domestic turmoil (the repossessed or broken furniture, the broken delftware) to convey a more universal 'state o' chassis' is, of course, a frequent device of the early plays, including *Cathleen Listens In*, where its use is more obviously allegoric and symbolic.

In *The Silver Tassie*, however, O'Casey organizes his symbols not simply into allegory, but into those rituals of communion and sacrifice which have always informed man's life, frequently on an unconscious level. For, in 'tr[ying] to go into the heart of war,'[18] O'Casey found himself exploring, through symbol and ritual, the often savage and merciless heart of man. The metaphor is one he uses in the autobiographies where, earlier, he had described 'the odious figure of war astride the tumbled buildings, sniffing up the evil smell of the burning ashes.'[19] Together, these two images reveal the outline of a recognizably human figure: it is the Croucher of Act II, a gigantic image of Man possessed by War, and so torn by despair and suffering that he is sick at heart. In *The Tassie*, then, the dominant theme of War is embodied in the Croucher, as well as being variously personified in certain other characters, but especially in Harry Heegan.

Who is it, one might ask, that has so elaborately arranged, in the bed-sitting room of the Heegan family, the symbols of Harry's victories, both in war and on the playing field? Mrs Heegan shows too little interest in such accomplishments to have given these symbols of his victories such a prominent display. And Sylvester, though he loves to boast about Harry's extraordinary feats, seems too permanently settled by the fire to have ever busied himself about the house. Likely it is Harry himself, probably with Susie's help, who has arranged the setting in anticipation of his triumphant return from the football field, as, certainly, it is Harry who will later use this same setting as a ceremonial altar to celebrate his victory.

In the meantime, both the medals on the purple velvet shield and the photograph of Harry in 'football dress' on the red-coloured stand symbolically represent, onstage, the eagerly awaited hero. For Harry's triumphant entrance, which does not occur until more than midway through Act I, has been carefully designed from the opening curtain. In this way, O'Casey has Harry's presence dominate the scene *even when he is absent*, a structure which is closely paralleled in Act II, so that – of all the characters – it is Harry who continues to dominate the play right through to the final exit.

The symbolic import of Harry's heroic stature becomes even more apparent when he is actually brought onstage carried upon the shoulders of his friends, though a closer look at the text reveals that O'Casey's original intention, at least before he saw Massey's Apollo production, which introduced this innovation, was simply to have the scene described by Susie:

> They're comin', they're comin': a crowd with a concertina; some of them carrying Harry on their shoulders, an' others are carrying that Jessie Taite too, holding a silver cup in her hands ...
>
> (... *Then steps are heard coming up the stairs, and first SIMON NORTON enters, holding the door ceremoniously wide open to allow HARRY to enter, with his arm around JESSIE, who is carrying a silver cup joyously, rather than reverentially, elevated, as a priest would elevate a chalice ...*)[20]

The origin of Harry's elevation onstage – an entry which is so right for the play it has since become a stage tradition (and one O'Casey must have agreed with) – is recorded by Stephen Gwynn, writing in the *Fortnightly Review* of the Apollo production: 'Then in comes the hero, carried by admirers ...'[21] Produced in this way, the scene is obviously much more dramatic, for, not only do we have Jessie's ritualized entrance carrying – 'as a priest would elevate a chalice' – the silver tassie from which wine is later drunk, but we have also the elevated body of the intended sacrifice, Harry Heegan, whose youthful, almost god-like figure, like the host, will be broken in the latter part of the play. The parallel elevations here help to underline, right from the beginning, the symbolic identification of the silver tassie with Harry, who has won the cup three times. Significantly, it is Harry who tells Jessie: 'Lift it up, lift it up, Jessie, sign of youth, sign of strength, sign of victory!' (p 26), for it is Harry who creates the ritual that is about to be enacted: a glorification of the mock war he has just won on the playing field and of himself, its hero. This 'war,' like the homefront battle of Teddy Foran and his wife, ironically prefigures the real war, in which the mock hero or god becomes the sacrificial victim. The parallel elevations also prepare for the sacrilegious smashing of the tassie in the second half of the play, where the depths to which Harry has fallen, crouched despairingly in his wheelchair, provide a striking visual contrast to the height to which he had risen, both literally and figuratively, in Act I.

Of even more significance than these two elevations within the first act, however, is Massey's elevation of the Croucher in Act II in the same area onstage in which Harry Heegan was elevated during the previous act. These parallelisms cannot help but work, perhaps subliminally at first, to provide some measure of unity between Acts I and II. Indeed, Massey's entire approach to the play, as described in his autobiography, reveals his imaginative and innovative response to the challenge of integrating, into the play as a whole, an act which 'at first reading ... appeared to be parenthetical,' but which he felt instinctively to be 'no interpolation but the core and substance of the play.'[22] Accordingly, Massey's innovative elevations, as we shall see, help to unify the play by clarifying the mysterious relationship between Harry, the Croucher, and the other soldiers.

For all the soldiers, as Susie makes plain, are participants in a diabolic ritual: 'The men that are defending us have leave to bow themselves down in the House of Rimmon, for the men that go with the guns are going with God' (p 29). Susie's reference to the House of Rimmon (2 Kings 5:18) ironically confirms the idolatrous context for the drinking of wine that Harry has just prepared, a mock communion that will be dramatically re-enacted in the final half of the play. This ritual, together with Harry's impassioned language and the images of field and virgin and gun, prepares for the battle zone scene of Act II, a flat landscape 'dotted with rayed and shattered shell-holes' (p 35), and for the actual arrival of the soldiers in the ruined monastery with its black-robed Virgin – the place where the elevated figure of the Croucher is the main participant in a stranger and more frightening ritual, the place where all the soldiers finally worship the gun.

Harry's mood and his words are reckless, and they veil the despair he feels at leaving life and love behind: 'Out with one of them wine-virgins we got in "The Mill in the Field," Barney, and we'll rape her in a last hot moment before we set out to kiss the guns! ... Into the cup, be-God. A drink out of the cup, out of the Silver Tassie!' (p 29). Here, the ritual drinking of wine from the tassie occurs twice: the first time Jessie participates in what is, in effect, a betrothal ceremony, a pledge to life and love; the second time – in anticipation of his future isolation – Harry drinks alone.

Ideally, the silver tassie, as we have seen, would be the Holy Grail.[23] In this context it would symbolize the purity and innocence of the heroic young man who has won it, and the righteousness of his quest. But the tragedy lies in the fact that, if the quest is not a righteous one, these virtues which have existed in Harry will be torn from him. Then, ironically, this ritual communion, as surely as the Black Mass of Act ii, will lead to destruction and sacrifice, for those who participate in the rituals of an unjust and godless war must be, in the final analysis, idolaters at the altar of life. And so, when Harry drinks from the cup alone, he unwittingly pledges his youth and strength, not to the service of life and love, but to the service of war.

As if in confirmation of this fact, and in preparation for Harry's departure, the lively and bright colours of the football hero, the play-warrior, the lover-of-life, are covered over by the drab khaki of the soldier's uniform. The transformation – the first of several to occur to Harry and the other soliders – is startling as Susie hands Harry his steel helmet and carries his rifle, as Mrs Heegan hurries her son into his topcoat, as Sylvester gives Harry his haversack and trench tools and carries his kit-bag. Clearly, the participation in the idolatrous communion is wholesale as all help in the ritual dressing and arming of the warrior for battle. Here, the expressionist choral chant, 'You must go back' (p 31), draws attention to the ritual even as it underlines the responsibility of its participants so that, as the words are picked up and elaborated on by the voices outside, 'Carry on from the boat to the camp ... From the camp up the line to the trenches' (p 33), we have a sense of an entire nation having blindly and selfishly dedicated itself – and its life and youth – to the senseless destruction of war.

The intrusion of the choral voices from outside dramatizes the larger forces that are operative and symbolically represents the impinging of blind fate or destiny upon the individual. But what we should also hear is simply the voice of the people expressing the will of the majority: 'They must go back.' The pronouncement appears to carry the force and weight of a categorical imperative, and it must be reckoned with, though its validity, throughout the rest of the play, will be called more and more into question. Here, the culmination of Act i of *The Silver Tassie* in an integrated expressionist choral effect, clearly anticipates the progression that becomes evident in the play as a whole: from the implicitly symbolic, heightened realism of the Dublin trilogy to the more formally organized (stylized) symbolism of ritual, a ritual which is nevertheless firmly embedded in reality.

O'Casey obviously felt that the technique was successful, for he uses it again, in a similar way, in the fourth act of *Red Roses for Me*, where a chorus comprised of the poor working men and women of Dublin claim Ayamonn as their leader – 'He comes with us!' – a claim that will result, finally, in his martyrdom. It is right that Ayamonn should answer the call, for there are some causes that must be fought and, if necessary, died for. But was the Great War one of these causes? Act II of *The Silver Tassie* makes clear that, in O'Casey's view, it was not.

As Harry and the other soldiers embark, the sacrifice which is about to be enacted is suggested by the slow moving away of the ship's masthead, which, throughout Act I, has formed a cross seen through the window above the altar at which the ritualized drinking of wine has taken place. And a life-size cross, whose Christ figure, like a wounded soldier, has an arm torn by an exploding shell, is one of the first images that demands our attention immediately following the curtain-rise of Act II.

THE CROUCHER

Among the ruins of a monastery, in the battle zone of the second act, the desecrated crucifix leans forward grotesquely, the Christ figure stretching out an arm as if in supplication to the Virgin. But the stained glass madonna, made 'vividly apparent' by lights inside the ruined monastery, is 'white-faced, wearing a black robe' (p 35), apparently unresponsive and uncaring. Here, the very absence of colour – the black and the white – suggests the sterility of the Church and its remoteness from man's life. Ironically, in this scene of desecration, the two figures become a parody of the pietà, even as the suffering figure opposite them – the soldier undergoing field punishment and tied, spread-eagled, to the great wheel of the gun carriage – becomes a parody of the crucifixion.[24] 'Underneath the crucifix on a pedestal, in red letters, are the words: PRINCEPS PACIS' (p 35). The inscription, in this context, is obviously intended to be ironic: the sacrifices being enacted are not to the greater glory of God, but, instead, make a mockery out of everything the Prince of Peace stands for.

Occupying a central position onstage, a big howitzer gun, with a long 'sinister' barrel pointing towards the front, symbolizes the machinery of war and War itself. Both are made by man and venerated by him, and the result of this idolatry, which has 'the Church's damned approval,' is man's physical and spiritual desolation. The ruined monastery, now used as a

Red Cross Station in which lie the dead and dying, suggests the Church's own desolate state. Unknowingly, the Church has become the House of Rimmon, a place of sacrilege.

The landscape stretching to the horizon is bleak and frightening: 'Here and there heaps of rubbish mark where houses once stood. From some of these, lean, dead hands are protruding. Further on, spiky stumps of trees which were once a small wood ... Across the horizon in the red glare can be seen the criss-cross pattern of the barbed wire bordering the trenches' (p 35). The visual impact, like that in a nightmarish landscape by Hieronymus Bosch, is staggering. Understandably, the scene evokes a litany of despair, intoned by the strange figure of the Croucher, whose own spiritual desolation is expressed physically in his worn and almost ghostlike appearance. Elevated on a ramp above the brazier, he seems larger than life, and, when the soldiers enter to huddle around the fire, his shadow hovers over them like the shadow of the Angel of Death.

A mass for the dying can be heard coming from a part of the ruined monastery, and the Kyrie Eleison provides a haunting response to the Croucher's ironic reversal of the words taken from the prophet Ezekiel:

> CROUCHER And the hand of the Lord was upon me, and carried me out in the spirit of the Lord, and set me down in the midst of a valley.
> And I looked and saw a great multitude that stood upon their feet, an exceeding great army.
> And he said unto me, Son of man, can this exceeding great army become a valley of dry bones?
> (*The music ceases, and a voice, in the part of the monastery left standing, intones*: Kyr ... ie ... e ... eleison. Kyr ... ie ... e ... eleison, *followed by the answer*: Christe ... eleison.
> CROUCHER (*resuming*) And I answered, O Lord God, thou knowest. And he said, prophesy and say unto the wind, come from the four winds a breath and breathe upon these living that they may die. (p 36)

As the Kyrie Eleison fades into silence, only to be replaced by the bitter responses of the disheartened soldiers, it becomes apparent that the ritual in which all now participate is a celebration, not of life, but of death.

This scene, with its stark visionary power rising so quickly from the opening curtain, is a tour de force of dramatic art, for the Croucher is O'Casey's strangest and most ingenious creation, deriving its inspiration initially from the Expressionist stage, yet going far beyond Expressionism in the complexity of its total achievement. Here, realism and symbolism mingle in a way that suggests affinities with Ibsen – with, for example, the Rat-Wife in *Little Eyolf*, whose entry betokens death. In the Croucher, then, we glimpse that most paradoxical of creations: a realistic figure of flesh and blood whose symbolic dimensions yet seem to take us into a realm beyond the natural world. Such a vision, in fact, can only be transfixed for a moment or two in time. Thus it is only during those moments, at the beginning of Act II, for instance, where the Croucher becomes the principal celebrant in an idolatrous communion, that we can sense a demonic spirit, at times a visible presence, hovering over all.

Of *The Silver Tassie* O'Casey wrote, 'I wished to show the face and unveil the soul of war.'[25] And, in the Black Mass of Act II, we actually have unveiled to us, in the mysterious figure of the Croucher, both the face and the soul of war. For, clearly, it is the demonic God of War that has possessed this despairing soldier. Throughout the rest of the act, until just before the end, he sits as motionless as an idol except for the illusion of movement created by the play of light and shadow across his face and body. In the flickering light, though there are moments in which the crouching form still looks like that of a sick and sleeping soldier, there are other moments in which we glimpse again the death's head, the horrible skull-like face of War. These transformations, which take place in the twinkling of an eye, are strange, but powerful. And while the stage action below may seem to call attention away from the Croucher, it is impossible to forget that he is there.

For when the soldiers enter and huddle together in a close mass over the brazier just beneath the ramp, they are clearly linked both aurally (by the chanting) and visually (by their stooped postures) with the Croucher above. Though their unwitting participation in the diabolic ritual seems spontaneous, it is somehow evoked by that dark and shadowy presence until, together, they become an image of a larger humanity, in which for the moment all individuality is merged.

Here O'Casey's complex mingling of realism and expressionism results once more in a number of strange and startling transformations as the individual soldiers of Act I 'dissolve,' in Act II, into the group of soldiers who are, for the most part, anonymous. In order to create these effects, O'Casey attempts a very specialized kind of doubling, which, as we shall see, is not unlike the kind Ernst Toller so frequently used. The only soldier who clearly retains his identity is – not Harry as we might have expected – but Barney. Tied to a gunwheel for stealing an Estaminay cock, he occupies a position onstage that immediately rivets our attention.

At the same time, there is a soldier in Act II who more gradually draws attention to himself, for he looks 'very like Teddy' (p 37). This soldier, as O'Casey must have intended, should be played by the same actor who plays Teddy, though ever since the Apollo production this doubling has, as often as not, been neglected in casting.[26]

Far from neglecting it, however, Massey apparently welcomed the suggestion and even went on to cast the actor who played Harry Heegan, Charles Laughton, as the 1st Soldier in Act II; though a statement in his autobiography indicates that he did so, not so much to satisfy the audience's wish to see Harry onstage again, as to realize what he understood of the play's expressionist structure, and so integrate Act II into the play on a symbolic, rather than on a realistic, level. He writes: 'Although the three soldiers from the first act appear in this scene, all the characters are ciphers and have no connection with the rest of the play.'[27] Massey's use of doubling, then, shows that his rapport with *The Silver Tassie* was such that he understood the thematic and symbolic relationship between Act II and the rest of the play: that war can strip man of his individual identity, and plunge him into a nightmare world where he is a robot-like part of a vast machine. But he remained unaware of the full potential of the doubling device to unify the play in terms of character and action, a unity which is essential if the ritual of war is to form an integral part of the play's vision.

In having a clearly recognizable character from Act I – Barney – appear in Act II, O'Casey is obviously identifying the scene as that part of the war zone to which the three soldiers have disembarked, as Mrs Foran says, 'safely' (p 34). But if Barney is here, and someone who looks very like Teddy, then where is their inseparable companion from Act I? where is Harry Heegan? Indeed, might not O'Casey be inviting the audience to ask this question? And do we not find ourselves searching for Harry, over and over again in the features of the other soldiers, as each face, in turn is lit up and momentarily distorted by the eerie red glow from the fire? Thus we anticipate Harry's arrival throughout Act II, much as we anticipated his triumphant entry, which did not occur until more than midway through Act I. In fact, Harry's absence from the beginning of both acts and the growing anticipation of his appearance further increases the parallelism between Acts I and II, a unifying device already strongly at work in the play.

Unfortunately, however, Massey's innovative doubling of the role of Harry Heegan and the 1st Soldier – the same actor in the same uniform – completed the needed recognition scene prematurely. The result, in the Apollo production, was that the audience recognized Harry at the beginning of the act and the unifying effect of parallelism was actually distorted. Certainly, of all Massey's innovations, this was the only one O'Casey did *not* incorporate into the Stage Version of the text, nor has it, so far as I am aware, ever been tried out again onstage.

And yet the idea of having Harry appear somewhere in Act II – preferably after the mid point of the act – is a fascinating one since, not only would it fulfill the expectations of the audience, but it would also answer, in a very concrete and practical way, Yeats' charge that, in *The Tassie*, 'there is no dominating character, no dominating action, neither psychological unity nor unity of action.'[28] The problem Yeats raises here has been such a difficult one that most O'Casey critics have continued to comment on it. Robert Hogan, for example, finds that, without Harry, Act II is undramatic; lyricism and 'stage magic' replace drama: 'the act is static, sheer mood. It depends for effectiveness less upon the dramatist than upon the set designer.'[29] His solution is drastic: omit Act II (and possibly Act III) from *The Tassie* altogether. By contrast, David Krause, whose pioneering work on O'Casey will always stand as a touchstone for later critics, takes a more positive approach. In keeping with the precedent set by the Apollo production, Krause suggests: 'Surely Harry is too important to be dropped completely. Perhaps there could have been a soldier "very like Harry," or possibly Harry, with his ukulele, could have been represented in distortion by a figure somewhat like the Croucher.'[30]

In fact, what holographs of *The Tassie* show is that Harry Heegan, at one point in the play's development, did appear quite recognizably in Act II,[31] and disappeared from that act as a realistic character only some time after the image of the Croucher began to shape itself strongly in O'Casey's mind in conjunction with the image of an anonymous, legless soldier. In the holographs, as these two images fuse, what we can see in the Croucher – in that wounded crouching soldier who participates in a diabolic ritual – is a soldier 'very like Harry,' or, rather, very like what Harry is to become.[32] But how to depict onstage the relationship between the symbolic Croucher and the realistic soldier, Harry Heegan, whose identity is now engulfed by war, remained an insuperable problem, one in which the decision of whether or not Harry should actually appear in Act II as a recognizable figure, or when he should appear, was critical.

The difficulty O'Casey had in solving this problem is further reflected in his treatment of Teddy, who also appeared originally in this act, like Barney, as a clearly recognizable figure. Yet Teddy's name was deleted from Act II in the very copy of the typescript that had been returned by the Abbey, as if this revision, in the face of Yeats' criticism, was somehow meant to validate Harry's continuing absence. Thus, when Teddy disappears he is replaced simply by an anonymous soldier. In a still later typescript,[33] however, O'Casey, having had time to consider the problem further, returned Teddy to the battle zone scene by adding the notation 'very like Teddy,' beside the first speech of the 4th Soldier. As we have seen, it must have been this stage direction which prompted Massey (while engaged in the practical expedient of reducing a large cast) to have the actor who played Teddy double as one of the anonymous soldiers in the second act – and to have the actor who played Harry double as the 1st Soldier.

In agreeing to this additional doubling in the Apollo production, O'Casey showed his willingness to experiment further with the idea of returning Harry, as well as Teddy, to Act II and so have all three soldiers there in some guise or other. But in failing to incorporate this particular doubling into the Stage Version of the text, O'Casey strongly indicated his recognition of the fact that this innovation was not working onstage. For what has happened to Harry and to the other soldiers can only be fully understood if the process of 'looking for Harry' is not interrrupted by a recognition scene which takes place much too soon.

In fact, with every entrance (and there is a lot of coming and going in this supposedly 'static'[34] act) we should be aware of looking for Harry. Though we do not find him, there are many things that remind us of him – the football game, for example, which suddenly erupts on mid-stage, occasioned by the brightly coloured ball that the frivolous Mollie has sent her soldier, 'To play your way to the enemies' trenches when you all go over the top' (p 51). The ball is red and yellow, the colours of life, the colours of Harry's football uniform. And so it seems, for an instant, in the midst of death, Harry springs to life, joyous, triumphant as we last saw him.

The effect of this scene, juxtaposed with the immediately preceding one, is electrifying. For, just moments earlier, comedy and pathos have modulated swiftly into terror as the soldier who has eagerly anticipated cigarettes or playing cards in the parcel from home receives instead:

3RD SOLDIER A prayer-book!
4TH SOLDIER In a green plush cover with a golden cross.
CROUCHER Open it at the Psalms and sing that we may be saved from the life and death of the beasts that perish.
BARNEY Per omnia saecula saeculorum. (pp 50–1)

At once, the solemn intoning of the Croucher's prayer and the Latin response chanted by Barney recall the way in which the act began. Again the Croucher assumes strange and inhuman dimensions, though, para-doxically, the crouching form continues, at the same time, to suggest man's mortal nature, humanity bowed beneath the shadow of a dark and menacing figure. It is in the shadow of death, then, that the gayly coloured ball bounces and the soldiers, who remind us of Harry and his joyous zest for life, begin to play – though not for long.

As the enemy's attack advances, and the soldiers prepare to defend themselves, the act moves swiftly to its conclusion in a further series of strange and frightening transformations, which, as in Harry's startling transformation towards the end of Act I from triumphant football hero to soldier, again involves both costuming and the physical movement of the actors onstage. When the soldiers put on their gas masks, 'their forms crouched in a huddled act of obeisance' to the gun – 'We believe in God and we believe in thee' (p 54) – they no longer look human.[35] There is something bestial about their appearance which recalls, and mocks, the Croucher's prayer 'that we may be saved from the life and death of the beasts that perish' (p 51). In fact, once the Croucher himself joins the sacrilegious worshippers of the gun, he can no longer be distinguished from the other soldiers, whose crouching forms now fill the stage. All have lost their identity, all have become less than human – anonymous links in the impersonal, and soulless machinery of war.

For what has just occurred, marked by that moment when the soldier crouched on the ramp descends to the stage below, is the final terrifying incarnation of the God of War, not in one soldier only but in all who, in their prayer to the gun, have willingly invoked his demonic spirit.

Yet, frightening as all these transformations are, there is one which is more terrifying still, for, in that exact moment between the time when the Croucher rises to come down from the ramp and before he reappears amidst the crouching forms of the other soldiers – the Croucher vanishes! And in the skull-like features of the despairing soldier who stands before us now, we should glimpse, instead, the drawn, anguished face of Harry Heegan, the missing soldier whose arrival we have so long anticipated. Then, before we can be quite certain of what we have just seen, the soldier puts on his gas mask, and there once again is the ugly, monstrous, terrifying face of War: the staring, empty eyes, the body deformed by the crouched posture, the voice chanting lifelessly in response to the corporal's hymn of praise to the gun.

To realize Act II onstage in this way, however, as part of an integrated narrative and symbolic structure, obviously requires one further innova-tion, one that the holographs and typescripts suggest, and that Raymond

Massey's Apollo production was actually moving towards: that is, the doubling of the roles of Harry Heegan, and – not of the 1st Soldier – but of the Croucher, himself. As we have seen, Massey's parallel elevations of Harry and the Croucher in the almost identical area onstage has already underlined their spiritual kinship, a relationship which is also confirmed by the fact that both are the main celebrants in a sacrilegious communion in which all the soldiers finally participate. These two sets of parallels, then, mutually reinforce each other to create a strong sense of the diabolic pattern that is weaving its way into Harry's life, one that – once it is thrust upon him – he will accept.

Seen in this way, on the level of character and action, as an integral part of O'Casey's haunting portrait of man possessed by the spirit of war, Act II of *The Tassie* is clearly meant to convey, not the physical, but the spiritual death of Harry Heegan. For it is important that we understand the nature of the terrible spiritual transformation that Harry undergoes in war, of which his crippled and impotent body, his permanently 'crouched' form, is but the exterior sign.

Here O'Casey's use of the mysterious figure of the Croucher to reveal what has happened to Harry Heegan recalls Ernst Toller's practice of revealing the inner, spiritual state of his protagonists by casting them in different symbolic roles. In *Masses and Man*, for instance, when he wishes to show the anguished feelings of guilt that the Woman (Sonia) experiences after she betrays her pacifist principles and joins actively in the revolution of the workers, Toller portrays her as a figure crouched motionless in despair and anguish, undergoing, in a purgatorial setting, the torments of the damned. Similarly, in *Transfiguration*, Toller has his protagonist, a soldier like Harry, appear in a great variety of symbolic guises, such as The Wanderer and The Prisoner.

To what extent O'Casey was consciously aware of the exact nature of Toller's experiments is difficult to say, but it is impossible to read either of these two plays without noticing that many of the images, symbols, and characters which O'Casey uses so economically in Act II of *The Tassie* seem to have come to him initially out of the plenitude of Toller's wild and extravagant imagination. For example, in the 'troop-train' scene of *Transfiguration*, certain elements of the setting seem oddly familiar: 'Badly burning oil-lamps shed a meagre, flickering light on the sleeping SOLDIERS huddled close together. With them one silent soldier (with FRIEDRICH's features) and another with a skull for a head: both shadowy figures' (p 66). When he conceived his own symbolic Croucher, did O'Casey have in mind, either consciously or unconsciously, the silent 'huddled' soldier and the one with 'a skull for a head,' as well as the anguished crouching figure

in *Masses and Man*? Was it partly the imaginative kinship of all those huddled and despairing creatures that allowed O'Casey to come up with an expressionist creation which was yet uniquely his own?

If the process was, in fact, a largely unconscious one, then this helps to explain why O'Casey did not indicate in the stage directions, as Toller undoubtedly would have, that Harry and the Croucher should be played by the same actor. On the contrary, in a letter to Lennox Robinson in which O'Casey assumes the Abbey will be producing *The Tassie*, he suggests a doubling of the roles, not of the Croucher and Harry Heegan, but of the Croucher and Surgeon Maxwell, a doubling which is sometimes carried out onstage.[36] Thus, we are forced to give some credence to that flat denial O'Casey made to Rollins in 1960: 'I never consciously adopted 'expressionism,' which I don't understand and never did.'[37]

Intent on taking into account the specific resources of the Abbey Theatre (and, by an irony of fate which the *Silver Tassie* controversy clearly underlines), O'Casey had inadvertently suggested a practice in casting that actually forestalled the one doubling of roles which would have immediately clarified the dramatic outline of the play itself. Nor does such an innovation require the alteration of even a single word of O'Casey's text. All it requires is the continuation of a practice which has been commonplace enough, both on the contemporary stage and earlier, but which had sometimes been used in a rather special way in Expressionist theatre.

The difficulties which *The Silver Tassie* continually encounters in production would seem to support these conclusions, and to confirm that a more innovative approach to the organic design of the play as a whole is a necessity. For the decision of whether or not the role of the Croucher and the role of Harry Heegan can be doubled effectively in the theatre – whether or not the production will actually 'work' – is one which can only be finally demonstrated onstage. Though it is clear that a decision to try out such an innovation should not hinge simply upon the conscious intent of the playwright, but rather upon the imaginative pattern which the play itself reveals.

What we notice in *The Silver Tassie*, then, is that, after Act I, when Harry is absent, the figure who dominates the stage in Harry's place is the Croucher, and, when the Croucher vanishes, Harry reappears. Both are figures larger than life; both have a symbolic as well as a realistic role, a role, moreover, which is identical: to show both the physical and the spiritual loss which man undergoes when he experiences war. And, in order to complete this overall design, what could be more natural than for Harry to reappear, not in the last half of the play only, but at that moment towards the end of Act II when the Croucher first vanishes? Not only would this one final innovation provide the solution to the problem Raymond Massey was struggling with in the Apollo production, 'the integration of this scene [Act II] into the play as a whole,'[38] but it would also prepare for the drastically altered role that Harry will play in Acts III and IV. Most important of all, this recognition scene would satisfy the expectations of the audience, who have been looking everywhere for Harry since Act II began, but who have, until now, been unable to understand the exact nature of the transformations that have been taking place.

In fact, from a practical viewpoint, it may be that the only way to show the kind of diabolic changes that have taken place, and so realize onstage the body of Harry Heegan possessed by the God of War, would be, as we have said, to have one actor play both roles. Then, throughout the act, there will, of necessity, be something about the Croucher – his build, the sound of his voice – which stirs memories of Harry almost imperceptibly within us until, when the recognition scene does occur, though we are initially startled, we feel, nevertheless, that it is right.

So far as the actor who plays this double role is concerned, he will no longer be left, during Act II, a mere passive backstage spectator of the very moods and passions which he will be called upon to embody so dynamically in Acts III and IV. Instead, he will have already portrayed, in the Croucher, the spirit of despair which seizes Harry, and will already have felt the spiritual death which has just occurred. He will then be able to understand what has happened to Harry to change him from the triumphant, joyous, and god-like young man of Act I to the despairing, inhuman, demon-possessed figure of Acts III and IV. With this understanding the depth of the portrait grows, and no longer should performances occur in which a superficial viewing of Harry is allowed to predominate.[39]

Moreover, as we go on to examine the last two acts, the structure of the play itself develops in a way which continues to suggest that this particular doubling – which both embodies and reveals the complex interrelationship of the two roles – would be a most effective way, not only of realizing in the theatre O'Casey's unique blend of realism and expressionism, but also of discovering the essential unity of *The Silver Tassie*.

THE JUGGERNAUT IN THE GARDEN

Act III reverses the process begun at the opening of the second act by 'dissolving out,' as it were, from the anonymous masses, the individual soldiers whose lives have been irrevocably reshaped by the tragedy of war. Thus, as well as being unified by recurring colour imagery, ritual, and the symbols of sacrifice, the last two acts develop from the previous two in terms of character and action: with the reappearance of Barney, not as sacrificial victim, as we might have expected, but as hero; of Teddy, now blind, and of the grotesquely transformed Harry, whose shattered spine confines him to a wheelchair. At first Teddy appears as an absurd 'stumblebum,' who inadvertently wounds Harry with words at every turn. But, by Act IV, he has come to terms with the dark world he now inhabits and, as a blind seer, helps Harry to that one moment of spiritual insight that marks the resolution of the play. As they leave, Susie tells us: 'Teddy Foran and Harry Heegan have gone to live their own way in another world' (p 103). Yet it is only with the exploration of the dimensions of that other world, and the tortuous route by which Harry reaches and finally comprehends it, that O'Casey's vision in *The Silver Tassie* is complete.

The last half of the play, therefore, shows us the harrowing of that hell which was revealed, in Act II, to be the destination of Harry and the other soldiers. As his name suggests, it is Harry[40] upon whom the chief burden of guilt, expiation, and atonement falls, though whether he will be capable of the task remains in doubt to the very last moment. The role which he must continue to play in this 'mass Passion' is developed within the context of the already established symbols, but is broadened now by the addition of the image of the garden.

As is so characteristic of O'Casey, symbols and images are made concrete, embodied in the stage setting, stage properties, make-up, lighting, and, of course, in the appearance and actions of the actors themselves. During the second half of the play, then, images of light and colour contrast the oppressive darkness of the war zone, a darkness which has been illuminated momentarily, however, by the red glow from the fire, and, by the 'white glare' from the silently firing guns. It is this white glare that is picked up in the intense surgical whiteness of the hospital ward in Act III, even as the fiery red is dominant among the brilliant colours seen through the arched entrance to the dancehall in Act IV. Both suggest the aftermath of war: the sterile, pain-filled existence of those who are crippled – and the apparently joyous and carefree life of those who seem to have come through war's holocaust unscathed. Though, in this way, the last two acts are diametrically opposed, each contains the symbols of sacrifice. For, in the hospital scene, the colours of war – black and red – are evident in the coverlets on the beds, while above, so that the wounded may pull themselves up, hang wooden cross-pieces. Similarly, in the Avondale club room to which the dancehall is adjacent, these same colours and shapes fuse in the overhead lanterns to form 'an illuminated black cross with an inner one of gleaming red' (p 80).

In the background of both scenes glass casements reveal a garden: at times a lost Eden, at times a Gethsemane where there is suffering and betrayal; and, finally, by the end of Act iv, perhaps a garden of promise and renewal, ever so faintly suggested by the green of the two sycamore trees. As the recurring symbols suggest, the structure of both acts continues to centre on the sacrificial victims of war, especially on Harry, whose angry, volatile presence continues to dominate the play. Though at times he is sunk in despair or momentarily elated by hope, too often Harry is caught up in a warlike rage that makes of him more a figure to be feared than pitied.

His entrance in Act iii – for, as usual, Harry is not onstage when the curtain rises – is a dramatic one, prepared for ironically by Sylvester's unintentionally prophetic words, 'how are the mighty fallen, and the weapons of war perished!' (p 58). No longer elevated triumphantly on the shoulders of his friends, but instead – as O'Casey clearly specifies in the stage directions – 'crouched in a self-propelled invalid chair,' Harry is the embodiment of that other isolated and despairing figure, the Croucher of Act ii, a transformation which will be dramatically re-enacted in the Juggernaut scene, more than midway through Act iii. The unexpected appearance of Harry trapped in the wheelchair should also recall, from the previous act, the equally unexpected appearance of Barney tied to the gunwheel, though, with the turning of the wheel of fortune, their destinies have been reversed. Here, the two images merge to form a composite one which is summed up now in the tortured person of Harry Heegan: man victimized by war and imprisoned by the machine becomes, finally, a symbol of all suffering and crucified mankind.

Harry's newly mechanized existence, marked by his incessant and purposeless movement onstage in the wheelchair – 'Down and up, up and down. Up and down, down and up' (p 58) – is a futile substitute for the movement of his own paralysed limbs and an expression of his rage and despair at what has happened. Significantly, the pain Harry suffers is mental, not physical, and is symptomatic of his spiritual desolation, a despair driven to an agonized pitch of intensity by the sense that no one understands what has happened to him, nor does he understand it himself.

In the visiting scene, the one person he so desperately wants near him is Jessie, but she is as terrified of what has happened as he is himself, and no one can make her come in from the garden, not even Harry, whose pathetic calling of her name is answered only by silence. The sense of Harry's tragic isolation is further underlined by Susie, who hurries in to clear the ward of visitors and order him to bed. The screen which Simon 'places around Harry, hiding him from view' (p 75), emphasizes even more the finality of Harry's separation both from Jessie and from everyone around him. The next moment, when the screen is taken away, we are startled by the transformation he has undergone, a transformation which denies Mrs Foran's empty words of comfort heard moments earlier – 'The drawn look on his face isn't half as bad as when I seen him last' (p 73) – and mocks Mrs Heegan's cheerful reply: 'Look, the hollows under his eyes is fillin' up, too.' For Harry's agony has etched a death-like pallor in his face and the black spread Susie has placed over him covers him like a shroud. As Susie turns off the lights in the hospital ward, leaving only the red light over the fireplace, the sudden oppressive darkness, in conjunction with the piteable image Harry now presents, as he struggles, with the help of the crossbar, into a sitting posture, once more abruptly realizes onstage the huddled, despairing form of the Croucher with his drawn, skull-like head.[41]

The components of the two scenes are parallel in structure: the elevated hospital bed with its dark covering occupies the almost identical area of the stage as does the Croucher's ramp in Act II;[42] the lighting – an eerie red glow permeating the ominous darkness – casts similarly grotesque shadows; and when, suddenly, the bell of the adjacent convent rings out for the last religious service of the day, we are reminded of the slow and stately notes of the organ in the ruined monastery which accompanied the Croucher's despairing prophesy of doom.[43] In fact, the deep, brassy tone of the slowly tolling bell accentuates the ominous note in Harry's words so that, as he speaks, we hear once more a prophecy of death and destruction: 'In a net I'll catch butterflies in bunches; twist and mangle them between my fingers and fix them wriggling on to mercy's banner. I'll make my chair a Juggernaut, and wheel it over the neck and spine of every daffodil that looks at me, and strew them dead to manifest the mercy of God and the justice of man!' (p 77)

Implicit in the reference to the Juggernaut – a metaphor which connotes the overpowering, destructive force of war – and realized concretely onstage by the menacing form of Harry crouched in the wheelchair, is the image of an idol carried by a chariot, beneath whose wheels the living are ruthlessly sacrificed. By Act IV where Harry literally 'make[s his] chair a Juggernaut' in which he runs into Barney and smashes through the glass doors of the clubhouse, we see in the misshapen, war-torn figure of Harry, not the idealized form of this god, but an image which accurately portrays his awesome and savage nature. As Harry's savage actions continue to strip him of all humanity, what we see, too, is an image of mechanized man: the inhuman, soulless, murdering force behind the impersonal machinery of war.

No wonder, then, that Harry's words repel Susie, for they denounce both man and nature and deny the possibility of mercy or justice. His wish to destroy the beauty of nature, to break the spine of every daffodil, even as his own spine has been shattered, means that Harry has brought the desolate landscape of the war zone back with him, an accurate reflection of his own spiritual desolation. In the absurd universe which he now inhabits, a world as senseless as the one Beckett's Hamm in *Endgame* wishes to destroy, Harry appears grotesque and his words ridiculous as he curses Susie, together with all living things: 'To hell with you, your country, trees, and things, you jibbering jay!' (p 77). Susie has no answer except for the stunned calling of his 'name' – 'Twenty-eight!'

Appropriately enough, in a godless world, in a world given over to the machine, Christian names are replaced by numbers and categories. Susie calls Sylvester and Simon, 'Twenty-six' and 'Twenty-seven,' and she reminds them, 'I am to be addressed as "Nurse Monican," and not as "Susie"' (p 60). Alternately, the patients are spoken of as 'poor devils,' a phrase which echoes ironically throughout Act III to point to the sometimes foolish, sometimes tragic, incarnations of demon-possessed man. The poorest devil of all, of course, is Harry, as his despairing cry, 'God of the miracles, give a poor devil a chance!' (p 79), makes plain. In the context of this ironic prayer, the Sisters' 'Salve Regina,' sung offstage like that other plea for mercy, the 'Kyrie Eleison,' should recall, from Act II, the terrible Black Mass which still threatens to separate Harry from life, and from God, forever.

Yet, terrifying as Harry is in Act III, he is even more terrifying in Act IV, which takes place at the Avondale Football Club, the place of his former triumphs. Everywhere he turns he is goaded into fury by the reminder of his bitter loss and vanished victories. His wrath, as he propels himself madly around the dancehall in pursuit of Jessie and Barney, is really a measure of his pain, though here Harry also appears as a figure of nemesis – one of the most familiar guises of War – seeking, in the absence of any other kind of justice, retribution and vengeance. And, in this guise, it is no wonder that Jessie cannot see the Harry she once loved. Certainly he can no longer be recognized in the crouched and frenzied figure who circles the dancehall again and again as if he and the machine are one entity, trapped in some senseless and destructive pattern of its own. What Jessie is fleeing from is not Harry, but the mechanized 'thing' that hurtles after her: the spectre of War, the Juggernaut beneath whose wheels she refuses to be crushed. And, of course, she is right.

The choice that Jessie has had to make is not an easy one, as is signified by her reluctance, at the end of the play, to join in the dance. Her cry, 'Poor Harry!' (p 103), is the only heartfelt expression of sorrow and pity that rises heavenward on his behalf throughout the play. The cry, like the pathetic flowers that she sends to Harry in Act iii, and which are flung so hopelessly on the black quilt at the foot of Harry's bed, as 'on a grave,'[44] suggests, too, her own sense of loss and grief. Of all the women in the play, she is actually the most sympathetic, and, in retrospect, she appears 'predatory' only if we believe the envious words of Susie and Mrs Heegan, or the vicious accusations of Harry, himself.

To Harry, Jessie is the sum of the life and love and joy that he has lost forever, a loss that becomes too great for him to bear when he sees Jessie in Barney's arms. In the grotesque quarrel with Barney which follows, Harry – exactly as he had promised – makes his chair a Juggernaut and bursts into the clubhouse from the garden to appear before Jessie and Barney like an avenging demon. Harry calls Jessie a 'whore,' and, as Barney bends over the wheelchair to seize him by the throat, these two crouching figures decorated with medals of honour become an image of all that is noble and god-like in man having been crippled and debased to the level of a beast.

Previously, during the ritual wine drinking which begins Act iv, Harry has seen himself, ironically, as a 'creeping thing' trying to praise the Lord, and demands: 'But stretch me on the floor fair on my belly, and I will turn over on my back, then wriggle back again on to my belly; and that's more than a dead, dead man can do!' (p 82). Implicit here is the image of a serpent, an image that suggests his own guilt. In this vivid context of a guilty and lost humanity, we should recall once more the bestial, crouching forms of the worshipping soldiers at the end of Act ii, with whom, to some extent, Harry's identity is still merged. Deliberately, as he did in Act i, Harry calls for the silver tassie so that it may be filled with wine. This time, however, Harry is aware of the true nature of that earlier communion, even as he is aware of the symbolic colour of the wine: 'red like the blood that was shed for you and for many for the commission of sin!' (p 92).

The phrase 'for the commission of sin' now clearly defines the earlier ritual as an idolatrous one. Yet Harry drinks again for, Christ-like, he has accepted the fact that this bitter cup will not pass away, but must be drunk to the full. Unlike Christ, however, he feels no bond of sympathy and love that would allow him to bridge the vast abyss separating him from man and from God.

The measure of the distance which separates Harry from others is shown in his frantic attempt to join in the revelry of the dancers, an attempt which fails partly because the dance itself, as the black streamers among the coloured ones suggest, is not a true celebration of life. Though often, especially in *Red Roses for Me*, O'Casey uses dance and song as a metaphor for that joyous celebration of life which is a truly sacred communion, the celebration here is clearly not of that nature. Instead, the scene is one of the most tortured in the entire play. As Harry, clad in a black suit and a red and black paper hat,[45] tries desperately to take charge of the revelries – 'Trumpets and drum begin! ... Dance and dance and dance' (p 93) – then madly whirls his wheelchair around to the tempo of the tune, there is a pathos surpassing anything achieved by the grotesque scenes of the Expressionists. At the same time, in its painful mingling of farce and tragedy, the scene also anticipates the metaphysical intensity so characteristic of the Theatre of the Absurd.[46]

Yet the scene goes beyond the Absurd, for, out of the bleak, metaphysical dimensions of the tortured landscape that Harry inhabits, a still, small voice is heard: 'Dear God, I can't' (p 93). Ironically, the cry is both a denial and an affirmation. It is the mark of a soul fallen by the wayside and desperately trying to struggle back to God. Teddy's hand on Harry's shoulder is the first sign that there will be any help on the journey, as, spontaneously, in balanced strophe and antistrophe, each carefully weighs the full measure of the lot that has been meted out to him, trying to see that the scales balance, that the measure is just:

HARRY I can see, but I cannot dance.
TEDDY I can dance, but I cannot see ...
HARRY I never felt the hand that made me helpless.
TEDDY I never saw the hand that made me blind.
HARRY Life came and took away the half of life.
TEDDY Life took from me the half he left with you. (pp 94–5)

Harry's crushing of the silver tassie, probably beneath the wheels of the Juggernaut (a scene which occurs offstage, as did the parallel one in which Harry was crippled), suggests his own role in the tragedy that has been enacted. As the chanting soldiers of the second act have warned us, God's children are 'self-slaying,' and now we have proof that the hand that is raised in war to strike a brother falls inevitably on one's own head. With this realization, despite the distorted form which now permanently veils his own humanity, he can ask once more to be recognized by God and by man:

> Dear God, this crippled form is still your child ... Dear Mother, this helpless thing is still your son. Harry Heegan, me, who, on the football field, could crash a twelve-stone flyer of his feet ... And now, before I go, I give you all the Cup, the Silver Tassie, to have and to hold for ever, evermore ... Mangled and bruised as I am bruised and mangled. Hammered free from all its comely shape. (pp 101–2)

The simplicity of his words speak movingly of Harry's new-found humanity and make good his plea for recognition, though, even as he speaks, his words become tinged with renewed bitterness at the thought of the terrible price he has paid. Moreover, the angry suggestion that the tassie be opened out again for Barney and Jessie indicates that, not only will there be other idolatrous communicants at the altar of life, but also, despite Harry's sacrifice, there will be other wars.

But for all the residue of bitterness and self-mockery, Harry's agony has lessened. He is no longer inconsolable, no longer totally isolated from those around him. Now, at last, he is able to accept the bond of love and comradeship that Teddy offers, and which is hallowed by their common suffering: 'Come, Harry, home to where the air is soft. No longer can you stand upon a hill-top; these empty eyes of mine can never see from one. Our best is all behind us – what's in front we'll face like men, dear comrade of the blood-fight and the battle-front!' (p 102) Together, they move into the garden, a place which is evocative, not of Eden so much as of Gethsemane, a place which, as it is set peripherally in opposition to the stark wasteland of Act II, and the absurd foregrounds of Acts III and IV, suggests the possibility, at least, of spiritual renewal.

For there is more than stoic endurance here: there is an understanding of the terrible suffering that man, in his blindness, brings upon himself, and in which he may unwittingly imitate the passion of Christ. Thus, as the dedication of the play makes plain – 'To Eileen with the yellow daffodils in the green vase' – there is, as always with O'Casey, in the face of suffering and death, a positive affirmation of life. If this affirmation in *The Tassie* comes as a whisper, rather than as a shout, it is because of the terrible intensity of the suffering. And if there is something more than faintly ironic, perhaps even quite absurd, about a Christ figure – Harry – who, though risen from his harrowing of hell, is only half-risen, and, therefore, impotent and powerless, there is also something incredibly audacious about the quality of the artistic vision which can bring us face to face with such a creation without leading us into despair.

'Personally, I think the play is the best work I have yet done. I have certainly put my best into it, & have written the work solely because of love & a deep feeling that what I have written should have been written.'[47] Though *The Silver Tassie* was fated to become his own private Gethsemane, O'Casey's letter to Lady Gregory makes clear the spirit in which the play was conceived and written, and the optimism with which it was sent forth. That its reception – and the resultant controversy – was so disastrous both for its author and for the Abbey Theatre is one of the greatest ironies in the history of modern drama.

For what O'Casey needed – and what Yeats refused him and Massey once gave him – was an experimental theatre in which to reshape and revitalize his plays onstage. In such a theatre, what *The Silver Tassie* can demonstrate is that it does not deserve to be thought of as a flawed masterpiece, but as a play which can finally overcome all flaws to achieve that perfection of form which is, and has always been, its birthright.

Oct. 14th 1929.

19, WORONZOW ROAD,
ST JOHNS WOOD,
N.W.8.

my dear Ray —
I am very glad that
you have found me a 'grand man
to work with.' God, I think has given
me the grace to know when I know,
& when I do not know. I have been
very comfortable and very happy
working alongside of your patience,
good humour, artistic vitality & skill.
I am very glad I came across a
man who was little of a high-brow &
much of a genius. And I hope that
English Dramatists will abandon their
faith — the do it was in the beginning, is
now & ever shall be, idea of Drama, &
give you — now & again, even — plays
that will give you a chance to "sing
a song & show the stuff you're made of."

Very Sincerely Yours,
Sean

Letter from Sean O'Casey to Raymond Massey, first director of *The Silver
Tassie. Private collection.* The 1929 Apollo production was one time when O'Casey
worked closely with his director. Their mutual appreciation of each other's
genius is evident.

Portrait of the cast, showing Harry elevated, from the Royal Shakespeare Company's production of *The Silver Tassie* at the Aldwych Theatre, London, September 1969. *Photo by Reg Wilson*

Scene from Act II of the Royal Shakespeare Company's production of *The Tassie* at the Aldwych in 1969. The Croucher stands in a crucifixion posture on a vertical plane above the gunwheel, thus underlining the parallel fate which has befallen the two soldiers. *Photo by Reg Wilson*

The Augustus John setting for Act II of C.B. Cochran's 1929 Apollo production in London, directed by Raymond Massey. *The Raymond Mander & Joe Mitchenson Theatre Collection, London*

TELEPHONE:
MAYFAIR 5858.

7, ST. ANDREW'S MANSIONS,
DORSET STREET,
LONDON, W.1.

Page from the 34-page holograph draft of *The Silver Tassie* which clearly shows that, at one point in the play's development, Harry Heegan appeared quite recognizably in Act II. (See p 35.) *Henry W. and Albert A. Berg Collection, The New York Public Library (Astor, Lenox and Tilden Foundations)*

Salutare tuum da nobis.

Clamor meus ad te veniat

gloria in excelsis Deo, et in terra pax

hominibus bonae voluntatis.

Page [52] of the holograph notebooks, v 6, showing the evolution of the figure of the Croucher in conjunction with the image of an anonymous, legless soldier. (See p 35 and pp 125–6 n32.) Parallel lines through a page indicate that it has been incorporated into a subsequent draft of the play. *Henry W. and Albert A. Berg Collection, The New York Public Library (Astor, Lenox and Tilden Foundations)*

Scene from Act II of the 1972 Abbey Theatre production of *The Silver Tassie*. Gas masks were used very effectively in this production. *Photo by Fergus Bourke*

Scene from Act III of the 1980 Abbey Theatre production of *Red Roses for Me*. The setting is the picturesque Ha'penny Bridge, just west of O'Connell Bridge. *Photo by Fergus Bourke*

3

Red Roses for Me

The defiant glimmer of hope in the midst of despair which rises, near the end of *The Silver Tassie,* out of the play's dark vision was destined to wait another fourteen years for its fullest and most complete expression in *Red Roses for Me.* Significantly, O'Casey's new visionary play also included a 'title' song, one that, in presenting an idealized viewing of reality, forms the thematic centre of the work out of which the expressionist framework derives. As in opera or symphony, symbolic motifs are introduced, elaborated upon, then dropped, only to be picked up again, varied, and at last woven into a final crescendo and resolution. For O'Casey had structured *Red Roses for Me* on the model of *The Silver Tassie*: three acts in which generally unacknowledged elements of expressionism mingle strangely with his basically realistic technique – and with the comedy which is never absent from his work – and one act whose visionary power at first seems to derive solely from Expressionist theatre.

What O'Casey had also done, as it turned out, was to use the potential for comedy, and the potential for the absurd, which some of the more extreme techniques of expressionism offered, and which had been almost completely unrealized by the predominantly serious and didactic drama-tists of the continental stage. From the down-to-earth vantage point of the Dublin slums, O'Casey recognized that man's struggle towards the infinite, never purely noble and romantic, is often very foolish. And it is when we forget this realistic viewing of ourselves that we are most in danger of becoming totally ridiculous. Yet it is impossible for man to live without his dreams, and, in his reaching towards the stars, he expresses something noble within himself, something truly god-like.

In *Red Roses for Me*, then, O'Casey's use of expressionism is unique because he is using it as a means of exploring man's relationship with the ideal. In fact, O'Casey found expressionism superbly able to convey those visions of heaven or hell which seem to arise spontaneously in the natural world when we come to grips with reality and struggle with the possibility or impossibility of realizing our dreams. Thus, in the 'homemade' expressionism of *Red Roses*, as in *The Tassie*, O'Casey continues to explore his tragi-comic vision of man.

Described somewhat enigmatically as 'perhaps the most popular play of what has been called O'Casey's "barren years,"'[1] *Red Roses*, because of its expressionism, has also, like *The Tassie*, suffered the charge of didacticism and disunity. A frequent distinction made by the critics (and one which makes clear the play's apparent lack of unity) is that the first half of the play 'is lively and engaging in O'Casey's early manner,' but that 'the second half goes overboard in a wallow of choric invocation by the Liffey and tear-jerking rhetoric on the steps of a church.'[2] Moreover, what such reviews make clear is that the problem of O'Casey's 'poetical'[3] language – the rhetoric which it is claimed he uses to convey his 'message' – is inseparable from the central problem of the success or failure of the third and fourth acts. But are these flaws in production, flaws which make the play seem a 'diffuse mixture of proletarian melodrama and lyric mysticism,'[4] a fault of the basic structure of the play itself? Or do they point instead to our continuing failure to understand the complex dramatic craftsmanship which reveals O'Casey's vision and his art?

In *Red Roses for Me*, a number of striking contrasts embody the conflict between the ideal world which Ayamonn envisions and the 'real' world of the Dublin slums. Light moves across darkness; a breathless calm stills the vibrant and gesticulating movement of crowds; grandiloquent poetry punctuates the raucous notes of everyday speech, until the harmony of song at last replaces discord. Characters are impelled wildly into life, gesture grandly or grotesquely for a moment, and are gone once more into silence. As effects of lighting, colour, and costuming help to create a series of transformations – some false, some true – the play becomes expressionist in the broadest sense, for all surfaces become luminous; all patterns of action, symbolic.

Though if we persist in looking only at the opposing surfaces the play presents, at 'the mannerism of colour – the external colour of names and sashes'[5] – or even at their strange juxtaposition, but not at their interrelationship and final union, *Red Roses* will continue to seem a jumble of colourful characters and events, an inexplicable mixture of styles, which defies all formal categories, all labels, including the one of 'romatic tragedy'6 in which it has most frequently been placed. In fact, only the term 'tragi-comedy' seems meaningful here, for it at least suggests something of the play's paradoxical and mysterious nature, expressed through the continual coming together of opposed and conflicting surfaces: of Ayamonn's royal crimson cloak – beneath which lies the padded hump – his bright green silk doublet, black working trousers, and heavy hobnailed boots.

Thus, the stage setting of *Red Roses for Me*, while returning to the realistic lower-working class milieu of the Dublin trilogy, suggests, in veiled symbols, much more than history or autobiography can explain. In the first half of the play, the horsehair sofa, like the one O'Casey's mother slept on, and the flowers, like those she tended in her 'little Garden of Eden,'7 link Mrs Breydon to the dramatist's own mother in a way which makes of Ayamonn's words, 'You gave me life to play with as ... a coloured ball' (p 135), a personal and moving tribute. As the play unfolds, however, Mrs Breydon's stature grows until she becomes an embodiment of Ireland's two symbolic mothers, both the black-shawled Kathleen and later, also, the blue-robed Madonna. Appropriately enough, then, it is the colours of her beautiful geranium and musk and fuschia, planted in the homely biscuit tins, that magically transform the rough wooden bench beneath the window into an altar of life – above which a cross formed by the transverse arms of a railway signal can be clearly seen. During the course of the action, this signal becomes a constant reminder of the railway workers' strike, a reminder that also hints at Ayamonn's mission and his sacrificial death – in that other role he will soon be called upon to play. As in *The Tassie*, where the mast of the ship on which Harry embarks forms a cross seen through the glass, there is a sense of the outside world – of history – impinging upon the individual, patterning his life in a way which he cannot entirely foresee or control.

The historical background of *Red Roses*, which eventually becomes a part of the action, recalls the 1913 Dublin strike, notably the clash O'Casey himself witnessed between the striking transport workers and the police, an event which took place in O'Connell Street on 31 August 1913. But O'Casey has the date of the action coincide with the Vigil of Easter, a fact which should bring to mind the Easter Rising of 1916 (itself prepared for by that earlier uprising) and the martyrdom of such heroes as Pearse and Connolly. Moreover, O'Casey actually wrote *Red Roses for Me* (1942) under the impetus of World War II, and, since he sets the time of the play as 'a little while ago' (p 126), there can be no doubt that he intends *Red Roses* to be viewed, not in the context afforded by the narrower perspectives of either history or autobiography alone, but in a context which is as timeless as it is contemporary.[8]

Within this larger perspective, Ayamonn's purpose to support the workers in their strike for an extra shilling a week is understood as a sacred mission, for, as Ayamonn explains at the end of the play, a shilling is 'our Shechinah' (p 211). The use of this symbol (drawn from Jewish religious art), in which the visible sign of God's glory is represented by rays of light coming down from heaven, explains the broad significance of the contrasting images of light moving across darkness that culminates in the sunset which transforms Dublin at the end of Act III, and of the golden-rayed suns on the breasts of the workers in Act IV.

In the first two acts, then, the irrevocable course of events which will set Ayamonn's feet on this dangerous path of transforming the world is carefully delineated. He tells Sheila, the girl he both loves and idealizes, 'my feet shall be where the redder roses grow, though they bear long thorns, sharp and piercing, thick among them!' (p 143). Thus, the motif of sacrifice – the first of three motifs of conflict established in Act I – is carried, not only by the image of cross and altar, but also by the symbolic imagery of roses and thorns which so often informs Ayamonn's speech, though he is careful to omit them from the ballad in which he sees Sheila as his Kathleen of the Red Roses:

A sober black shawl hides her body entirely,
Touch'd by th' sun and th' salt spray of the sea;
But down in th' darkness a slim hand, so lovely,
Carries a rich bunch of red roses for me. (p 150)

Here, the symbolic red roses, associated traditionally with Christ's passion – and later in the play with Ayamonn's – becomes associated also with the ideals of Ireland's past, for in the title song, as David Krause has noted:

The black-shawled woman ... is Ireland, a Kathleen ni Houlihan of the Dublin slums offering her red roses as the token of a new life for her people. Ayamonn creates this vision of her in his song as in a dream; and the action of the play grows out of his struggle to merge the real and the ideal Kathleen.[9]

But it is only as Ayamonn's vision is resisted that it grows stronger, only as Sheila's practical nature opposes being made into 'a spark in a mere illusion' (p 143), that Ayamonn sets out courageously on that course of action which will lead, inevitably, to his death. Though before that final transfiguration occurs, the Ayamonn that we see at the beginning of the play, who is so ridiculously idealistic and impractical, must be transformed into a 'practical Dreamer,'[10] one who is able, not only to inspire the strikers, but also to lead them.

That the transformation which Ayamonn has been trying so stubbornly to effect – as he rehearses a Shakespearean scene for a benefit in aid of the strikers – is a false one, bearing no relationship to the needs of the Dublin poor, is suggested by the padded cape which gives Ayamonn the grotesquely hunchbacked form in which he first appears. The deformity itself makes plain how 'ill-suited' are his plans to help the strikers, a fact which is underlined by his naïve belief that the strike, in any case, will not occur. Ironically, however, Mrs Breydon is quite aware of the real threat the strike poses, even as she is aware of all the other conflicting forces which threaten Ayamonn from within, as well as from without. And yet, earlier, we have seen her so caught up in Ayamonn's world of 'make-believe' that, for the moment, her sound common sense has deserted her altogether, and she allows the door of their usually hospitable home to be barred shut against friend and neighbour alike. The 'real' world must, at any cost, be prevented from breaking in upon them, for when it does it will shatter the illusion of colour and beauty which Ayamonn has been struggling to create in the midst of the Dublin slums.

Mrs Breydon sees Ayamonn's passionate devotion to art and poetry as something which is itself impractical because it is undermining his health and pulling his life apart. For, though Ayamonn's love of beauty is sincere enough, his artistic talents fall far below his aspirations, as Roory's frank question makes all too plain: 'What kid was it sketched th' angel on th' wall?' (p 157). And Ayamonn, like O'Casey himself, admits, 'I'd give anything to be a painter.' Nor, with the exception of the song 'Red Roses for Me' (which appears in the fictionalized autobiographies as a ballad of the Dublin streets), is Ayamonn much of a poet.

Here, in fact, is the whole point of the rhetorical, sometimes even bombastic, language which the play, to the despair of its critics, contains. At times the language invites criticism, not of O'Casey, but of Ayamonn, and of Ayamonn only *as* poet, for his noble sentiments will be validated by his noble deeds before the play is done. In this respect Ayamonn is quite unlike Davoren, that earlier and more satirical self-portrait that O'Casey creates in *Shadow of a Gunman*. Though Davoren claims, with Shelley, that 'The poet ever strives to save the people' (p 127), he refuses to risk his life – even for Minnie – and so is unable to translate into action the many fine ideals in which he professes to believe. Whereas Ayamonn's 'gold canoe' speeches (perhaps the most outrageous examples of rhetoric in the play) are linked by their colour imagery to the transformation scene of Act III and are a foreshadowing of Ayamonn's death in the service of his ideals. Such a use of language, with its multiple dimensions and ironies, goes far beyond realism to become expressionist in a special way, for it is deliberately reaching, at one and the same moment, both towards the absurd and towards the sublime. It is O'Casey's 'homemade' expressionism, then, that often makes the language comically 'poetic' when characters feel the influence of Ayamonn's presence, or else when they, too, are inflamed by their passion for the ideal.

Caught up in the vision of his song in which he sees Sheila as both the real and the ideal Kathleen, Ayamonn denies her angry accusation: 'you think more of your poor painting, your poor oul' Ireland, your songs, and your workers' union than you think of [me].' He tells her: 'You're part of them all, in them all, and through them all; joyous, graceful, and a dearer vision; a bonnie rose, delectable and red' (p 144). Ideally, what Ayamonn says is true, though Sheila's stubborn refusal even to listen to the song, 'Red Roses for Me,' which Ayamonn is now struggling to bring onstage, suggests that reality has an odd way of resisting both the dream and the dreamer.

How difficult it is to transform the world with a song is further suggested by the comic struggle which ensues when Brennan, who has composed the music for 'Red Roses,' finally does manage to gain admittance, bringing the reluctant Sammy with him. Though Sammy is finally persuaded to sing, and he does manage to finish the song despite the constant interruptions, there is absolutely no effect of either singer or audience having been transformed by the magic of words and music. On the contrary, the very lifelessness of the ideal when it bears no relationship to the lives of the people is underlined in an intentionally comic way by O'Casey's sudden and unexpected juxtaposition of one of the more extreme techniques of expressionism with the realism of the Dublin tenement. The 'pale and mask-like' face of the singer, together with the brilliant colours of his costume, should set him apart from the everyday world so that, as he sings, the words, too, should have a dream-like and lifeless quality. Nor is this effect uncalled for, since Sammy's self-effacing nature and his 'resignation to the world' (p 148) and to his fate, are, of course, the very opposite of Ayamonn's courage – one very important quality needed to realize the ideal. But while Ayamonn has the courage to oppose Sheila's viewing of him, he is helpless to make her understand. The song must be heard by Sheila for she is in the song, and, as she listens so reluctantly with her back to the singer, and Sammy so shyly sings with his back to the audience, the real and the ideal are but a few paces apart. Here, Ayamonn's inability to fuse the idealized world he imagines with the dissonant reality about him differs sharply from the miraculous transformation which he will be able to evoke in Act III.

In this situation, Ayamonn's rather comic helplessness is actually symptomatic of the internal conflict which he feels, and which finds its expression in the 'lovers' quarrel' motif that punctuates the first two acts of the play. Religious differences are not the real basis of Sheila's concern, a concern that is merely hinted at in Act I when she tells Ayamonn: 'We must look well ahead on the road to the future. You lead your life through too many paths instead of treading the one way of making it possible for us to live together' (p 143). Her practical words have the rhythms of prose, as Ayamonn's romantic image of the rose-strewn 'way' is reduced to platitude, and her repeated admonition, 'be serious,' moves dissonantly across Ayamonn's impassioned and lyrical outbursts.

The total failure of the lovers to come to any kind of agreement, either here or in the following act, is itself a reflection of the divisive forces at work everywhere in Ireland, forces which frequently impinge upon and prevent the fulfilment of purely personal destinies. Mrs Breydon has already warned her son: 'The bigger half of Ireland would say that a man's way with a maid must be regulated by his faith an' hers, an' the other half by the way her father makes his livin'' (p 134). The lives of the lovers are so bound up in the religious, political, and economic issues which divide the country that there is really no way the threads can be untangled.

Similarly, each of Ayamonn's friends represents a thread of the tangled fabric which is Ireland rent by discord. Their quarrelling, together with that of the lovers, is the second motif that becomes dominant in this half of the play. Each friend, too, provides a colourful and comic contrast to the other so that the combined effect is of an irrepressible vitality spilling out on to the stage. Yet each character also has a 'speech tag' – such as, Roory's 'Sword o' Light' (p 159) – a device O'Casey could have adopted either from Ibsen or Strindberg, and which, as it is used here, tends, for the moment, to turn character into caricature, and to suggest that narrowing of humanity which results when one's viewing of the world is too single-minded.

At the same time, however, the complex duality of man's nature is often taken into account by the names O'Casey gives his characters: for example, Brennan Moore, the tenement landlord who wants more and more money is also Brennan o' the Moor, who, like his legendary namesake of the Irish ballad, gives money to those who are in need. There is an added complexity in this 'Robin Hood' aspect of Brennan's character, however, since he is accused of robbing, not the rich, but the poor. With Brennan, then, there is an ironic elaboration of the third dominant motif – the motif of theft.

Naturally enough, both the Protestant Brennan and the atheist Mullcanny immediately fall under suspicion when, at the end of Act I, the statue of the Virgin, Our Lady of Eblana, disappears mysteriously from her niche in the hall. In any case, whoever is to blame for the statue's disappearance, there is a growing sense, conveyed largely by the despairing voices of the chorus of Dublin poor, both here and in Act II, that the divisive forces at work in Ireland are somehow responsible for robbing the people of whatever 'wealth,' either material or spiritual, they might once have had. Together with the cross formed by the railway signal, the statue of Our Lady of Eblana (carried by the poor in ritual procession) embodies the economic and religious forces that have been at work in Ireland for centuries and are now entering directly into Ayamonn's life. As the poor appear at intervals in the doorway of the Breydon home, there is a sense of their plight impinging upon Ayamonn's life in a way which can no longer be ignored.

Ayamonn's broad humanity, as his name suggests (Ay-a-monn or Everyman), struggles to resolve and contain all these opposing forces which are embodied so strongly in the narrower humanities of all his wildly gesticulating friends. Ayamonn defends Brennan, gently silences the mocking Mullcanny, and promises to look for the stolen statue. He is as generous now to the poor people who have come, uninvited, into his home as he was selfish before, at the beginning of the act, to all those he would not admit. The transformation is a magical one and is symbolized by the gradual shedding of the colourful hunchbacked cape of Gloucester (p 135), and the green silk doublet (p 156); and by the donning of the drab oilskin leggings, coat, and sou'wester (p 157), which is the 'costume' in which he must face the dark and rainy workaday world.

Previously, Mrs Breydon had made a similar transformation, shedding the rich blue velvet cloak with its silver lace, 'lest it give me gorgeous notions' (p 135), for the thin, black shawl[11] in which she goes to minister to the needs of a sick Catholic neighbour. Clearly, the earlier transformation to nobility, as was the case with Ayamonn, has been a false one, for, while robed in the royal blue and silver, she has been behaving ignobly and selfishly; whereas, in the 'costume' which she wears everyday, her true or inner nature as the black-shawled Kathleen is revealed. Ayamonn had spoken irritably of her then as 'an imitation sisther of charity' (p 138), forgetful, for the moment, that beneath the darkness of her shawl are hidden qualities of true nobility, compassion, and self-sacrifice, those very qualities which the red roses of his song suggest but which Sheila, as yet, does not understand. Thus there is a strong suggestion – conveyed largely by the use of costumes and colour symbolism – that the ideal is actually hidden within the darkness of the everyday world.

When, at the end of Act I, Ayamonn goes out into the darkness carrying the shunter's lantern, there is a sense that, like a romatic counterpart of the cynical Diogenes, he is going to look for these ideals in the dark world around him.

THE OPENING OF A DOOR: HISTORY AND THE INDIVIDUAL

Throughout the second act, the motifs of conflict which have been established in Act I become more fully articulate. The motif of quarrelling, for example, carried by the raucous voices of both lovers and friends, modulates abruptly into the shattering sound of stones breaking through glass – a sound which can be heard again in Act IV. It is this 'speaking image' of Ireland divided, and at war, which demands to know who is the real enemy and what are the real battle lines to be drawn. Similarly, the motif of theft continues to pose the puzzling question of what has really been stolen and by whom, as the dissonant note struck by the hymn to the newly regilded Lady of Eblana (returned now by Brennan to her niche in the hall), signifies a tentative and oddly false resolution to the problem of the missing statue. In any case, it is gradually becoming clear that what has really been stolen must be returned if ever the quarrelling which rends Ireland is to cease. How this can best be accomplished is suggested by the partial vision of the Fenian song in which Ayamonn joins at the end of Act I, and is articulated more fully, in Act II, by Ayamonn's vision of 'a song all men can sing.' Here, the motif of sacrifice, subtly suggested by the image of the 'palm branch,' carries the theme of Ayamonn as 'saviour.'

All these motifs, together with the conflicting and intermingling imagery of light and darkness, point to that inescapable duality which is the very basis of our humanity. The resulting conflict of often narrow and limited viewpoints, externalized and made concrete onstage in the rowdy, argumentative figures and angry voices of Ayamonn's friends, culminates now in an image of Ireland at war. Roory, the Catholic Nationalist, clashes with Brennan, the Protestant Royalist, and both clash with the Atheist, Mullcanny. All the while, the Poor clash with the Rich (and what an odd representative of the wealthy Capitalist O'Casey provides us with in Brennan), as alliances are formed, then dissolved, in the twinkling of an eye, depending upon which enemy is foremost. The stage erupts in fierce verbal duels in which each defends his own beliefs and maintains his own viewing of the world against all others. And throughout, the calm voice of Ayamonn strives to make itself heard in defence of yet more ideals – Truth and Freedom! 'Let us bring freedom here, not with sounding brass an' tinkling cymbal, but with silver trumpets blowing, with a song all men can sing, with a palm branch in our hand, rather than with a whip at our belt, and a headsman's axe on our shoulders' (p 169). The kind of freedom which Ayamonn envisions is far more revolutionary than that understood by Roory with his fanatic wish to free the Irish from English domination. Yet so long as Catholic and Protestant fight their skirmishes on the grounds either of a dogmatic religious faith or of an equally blind patriotism, then the real battle against those who refuse economic, and spiritual, liberation to the poor will never be fought.

Earlier, Mullcanny had tried to make Brennan and Roory understand that interests which should have nothing to do with religion may underlie the strife that is pulling their country apart: 'You pair of damned fools, don't you know that the Pope wanted King Billy to win, and that the Vatican was ablaze with lights of joy afther King James's defeat over the wathers of the Boyne?' (p 166). The implication, introduced here and developed in the last half of the play, is that the real enemy is neither Catholic nor Protestant, but the powerful Authority – Kafkaesque in its terrifying anonymity – that is wielded, paradoxically, in the name of both churches, and of the state as well. It is in the selfish interests of this unenlightened Authority that the poor be kept poor so that the wealth of the country can remain in the hands of those who already possess it. Moreover, when the Catholic workers are led by the Protestant Ayamonn, and the strike itself has the blessing of the Protestant minister, it becomes even more apparent that what is dividing Ireland is perhaps not so much a religious issue as an economic one.

Similarly, as the 'lovers' quarrel' motif develops, it is impossible for

Ayamonn to remain unaware that it is not simply religious differences which divide him from Sheila. In coming to see Ayamonn, Sheila has already defied her parents and her church, but she will not, at this point in the play, defy the authority of the Inspector, who, though he does not yet appear, is just beginning to make himself felt as a powerful and threatening presence. The real choice Sheila offers Ayamonn is couched in the practical language of the workaday world: 'You will either have to make good or ... lose me' (p 172). It is this painful choice which, in Act ii, precipitates the growth of Ayamonn's character so that the practical and idealistic sides of his nature are at last united.

Sheila has rejected the vision Ayamonn has of her as the beautiful Kathleen ni Houlihan: 'Now, really, isn't it comical I'd look if I were to go about in a scanty petticoat, covered in a sober black shawl, and my poor feet bare!' (p 171). Yet, ironically, a transformation of sorts has taken place, for when Sheila tells Ayamonn that he can be made a foreman if only he will divide himself from 'the foolish men' in the coming strike, his furious answer makes plain that, in Ayamonn's eyes, she has become, not a true, but a false, Kathleen: 'D'ye know what you're asking me to do, woman? To be a blackleg; to blast with th' black frost of desertion the gay hopes of my comrades ... Oh, Sheila, you shouldn't have asked me to do this thing!' (p 172).

The scene mingles irony and pathos in a typically O'Caseyan fashion, since the love that Ayamonn and Sheila have for each other is genuine enough, though the divided humanity which struggles to realize this love is no match for the forces which are ranged against it. These forces are embodied now in the violence of conflicting beliefs which rage both within the tenement and without. And the inevitable riot which has erupted offstage as the outraged Catholics kick and stone Mullcanny for his heretical views parallels the violence of emotion felt by Sheila and Ayamonn as their lives are wrenched apart. The climax of their quarrel and the meaning of Ayamonn's decision to support the strikers is underlined by the entrance of Mullcanny, dishevelled and bleeding, followed by the crash of stones and the sound of glass breaking. These events mark the entry into Ayamonn's life of a violence which can no longer be contained by words alone.

But if the irony of the human condition is inescapable, rather than have us despair totally, O'Casey would have us laugh at its absurdity. The uproarious scene that follows, in which Brennan, Roory, and Mullcanny crawl around on their hands and knees to avoid the stones crashing through the windows, is a comic acknowledgement of that cruel and absurd universe which is always threatening us – and our beliefs – with extinction:

> MULLCANNY (*pityingly*) Bullied be books – eternal facts – aw! Yous are all scared stiff at the manifestation of a truth or two. D'ye know that the contraction of catharrah, apoplexy, consumption, and cataract of the eye is common to the monkeys? Knowledge you have now that you hadn't before; and a lot of them even like beer.
>
> ROORY Well, that's something sensible, at last.
>
> BRENNAN (*fiercely*) Did they get their likin' for beer from us, or did we get our likin' of beer from them? Answer me that, you, now; answer me that!
>
> ROORY Answer him that. We're not Terra Del Fooaygeeans, but sensible, sane, an' civilized souls.
>
> MULLCANNY (*gleefully*) Time's promoted reptiles – that's all; yous can't do away with the os coccyges!
>
> BRENNAN Ladies present, ladies present. (p 175)

As in the final scene of *Juno and the Paycock*, this 'state o' chassis' in which man continually finds himself is quite real, suggesting as it does both the disintegration of a personal world, and, reflected in it, the disintegration of a world order. However, on the most universal level, the 'state o' chassis' is even more exact: it is that dark, primordial chaos out of which creation first sprang and into which it is always threatening to return. Mullcanny, we are told, 'would rip up the floor of Heaven to see what [is] beneath' (p 169), and what is beneath surprises even Mullcanny. It will surprise Ayamonn, too, for it is on this larger plane of action that Ayamonn's struggle with the powers of darkness is now about to unfold.

Try as he may to keep these dark forces without so that he may deal with the world solely on his terms, Ayamonn has found that the world is forever breaking in upon him and insisting that he meet it face to face. He has come a long way from his position in Act I where he tells his mother that he has little to do with the strike: 'I'm with the men, spoke at a meeting in favour of the demand, and that's all' (p 132). Now his commitment to the strike is absolute: symbolically he burns the 'warrant of warning' (p 181) sent by the Authorities and promises the Railwaymen that he will address the strikers. With this firm decision, Ayamonn realizes that 'the Minstrel Show must be forgotten' (p 183), and the transformation to 'practical Dreamer' is complete. For Sheila has thoroughly disillusioned Ayamonn of the possibility of realizing, through words alone, the vision of his Kathleen of the Red Roses. Instead, by his courageous action of leading the striking railwaymen, Ayamonn will attempt to translate into reality his dream of a Kathleen ni Houlihan who is, not only beautiful, but true.

The two Railwaymen who have come directly to Ayamonn for help are the last of a long series of petitioners at the Breydon door. Significantly, Eeada ushers in both the Rector and the strikers, and this ceremony, together with the murmur of prayer from the hall, suggests that the whole impetus of the play, from the time the Breydon door was first reluctantly opened, has been converging upon this moment. Once more, as with the entrance of Sammy in Act I, O'Casey goes beyond the heightened realism so characteristic of the early masterpieces to employ in an equally complex way some of the more specialized techniques of expressionism. Thus the Railwaymen are designated by number, rather than by name, and are linked by their dark clothing and mask-like expressions to the anonymous masses of Dublin poor. The mask-like faces, so expressive of the plight of the Railwaymen and of their 'resignation to the world,' are intended to convey, like the masks of Greek tragedy taken over in various ways by the Expressionists,[12] a sense of the fate of the individual, and of the inevitability with which, unless other destinies intervene, he will be drawn towards it. When Ayamonn does call the 1st Railwayman by name, there should be a sense of the personal impinging upon the impersonal forces which have otherwise robbed the Railwaymen of both their identity and their freedom.

This 'theft,' so similar to the one the Dublin poor have undergone, has had the same result: all colour and beauty have faded from their lives, and they, too, are part of a world of darkness, a fact which is substantiated by the expressionist use of colour and clothing symbolism throughout the first half of the play. For the 'drab' clothing of the Railwaymen, like the 'drab brown' suits of the men and the 'chill grey' dresses of the women, each with their 'faded blue, red, green, or purple [patches]' (p 137) – or like Mrs Breydon's black shawl, or the dark mackintoshes of Ayamonn's friends, or Ayamonn's drab oil skins – makes them all recognizably part of that dark world of toil and grime and poverty which they inhabit.

The poor working men and women of Dublin do, in fact, play a larger role in *Red Roses for Me* than is usually recognized. This role, in the first half of the play, is, for the most part, enacted on the periphery of the stage, though in Act III it will become a part of the central action. In order to give emphasis and definition to this role and so integrate it with the main action, O'Casey once more employs a technique of expressionism: the ritualized choral procession in which the statue of Our Lady of Eblana plays the most important part.

'Eblana' is an earlier name for Dublin, and the statue 'is wearing a crown that, instead of being domed, is castellated like a city's tower, resembling those of Dublin' (p 137). Thus the statue is a particularly Irish Madonna, a composite figure of Ireland's two ideal symbolic mothers, the Blessed Virgin and Kathleen ni Houlihan. Maureen Malone, writing in *The Plays of Sean O'Casey*, is the first to recognize some of the implications of this association: 'The bedraggled figure, the "Lady of Eblana's poor," is in fact Dublin herself, before the transformation which takes place during the vision of the [third] act.'[13] Moreover, the faded colours of the statue, which 'was once a glory of purest white, sparkling blue, and luscious gilding,' together with the fact that 'the pale face of the Virgin is sadly soiled by the grime of the house' (p 137), serves to link the statue, more particularly, with the plight of the Dublin poor.

A passage from the autobiography goes a long way towards corroborating the ironic context in which this association of the faded statue with Dublin and her people must be understood. O'Casey writes:

Frequently he wandered, hurt with anger, through these cancerous streets that were incensed into resigned woe by the rotting houses, a desperate and dying humanity ... the few little holy images they had, worn, faded, and desperate as the people were themselves; as if the images shared the poverty and the pain of them who did them reverence. Many times, as he wandered there, the tears of rage would flow into his eyes, and thoughts of bitter astonishment made him wonder why the poor worm-eaten souls there couldn't rise in furious activity, and tear the guts out of those who kept them as they were.[14]

Here, O'Casey's anger makes plain that he sees in the faded 'holy images' symbols of what the alliance of religious, political, and economic forces have done, not only to Ireland and her people, but also to the Church herself.

The statue of Our Lady of Eblana, then, like the picture of the Virgin in *Juno*, is totally ineffective as the source of help and comfort she is meant to be, a fact which is doubly underlined as the Catholic women tend to the washing of the statue while the Protestant Mrs Breydon braves the wind and the rain to care for, and comfort, a dying Catholic neighbour. The ironic context in which O'Casey often sees Ireland's two symbolic mothers is clearly summed up here, though much of the irony should be evident from the time we first see the Dublin poor appear with the statue onstage: 'All their faces are stiff and mask-like; holding tight an expression of dumb resignation; and are traversed with seams of poverty and a hard life' (p 136). The mask-like faces of both men and women show them to be, like the masses of Dublin poor everywhere, trapped within a fate which is somehow indissolubly linked to the statue they are carrying and to the religious and nationalist forces which it represents. They walk in 'a kind of simple procession' (p 137), and their stylized movements onstage, together with their chanted choric responses, show that their lives are controlled and shaped by these forces. The women's faces reveal that every stage of life from youth to age is the same endless round of hardship, and there can be no escaping the grime and toil and poverty which makes up the substance of their lives.

Eeada 'directs' the course of the action, but its development only suggests the futile role in which the Dublin poor are cast. They, too, are trying to work a transformation of sorts, trying to remove some of the grime and return some of the colour to Our Lady of Eblana. But they must first borrow the soap from a Protestant neighbour and, even then, as Eeada admits, 'it's th' washin' that's done away with the bonnie blue of th' robe an' th' braver gold of its bordhers an' th' most o' th' royalty outa th' crown' (p 137). Moreover, the story Eeada tells of little Ursula, who saves her pennies to have the statue regilded only to find that 'whenever she's a shillin' up, it's needed for food an' firin',' also reflects the inability of the poor to change the course of their lives in any significant way. Ursula is the only child in the play, yet she seems most unchildlike and joyless in her obsession to care for and venerate the statue.

Stranger still is the effect on the people of the statue's disappearance. If the statue has not been stolen by one of the Protestants in the house, then the poor Dubliners are all too ready to believe that Mullcanny's diabolic influence has caused Our Lady of Eblana to come down 'of Her own accord' (p 155) from her niche in the hall and slip away. This element of irrational fear points to the fact that the Dublin poor cling to their faith in an unenlightened and superstitious way. Though ostensibly their search for the statue is motivated by the love they have for their 'sweet Lady of Eblana,' there is actually a strong sense of nemesis descending:

CHORUS Our Lady of Eblana's gone!
SINGLE VOICE An' dear knows what woe'll fall on our poor house now. (p 154)

And once the statue is found, newly regilded, and returned mysteriously to her niche in the hall, the people's response is even stranger, for what is most noticeable is the 'frozen look of resignation,' the joylessness which is the odd accompaniment to what we would expect to be an occasion for celebration. The song which the people sing strikes a dissonant note, for it is neither a hymn of praise nor of joy, but, instead, is a mournful appeal to the Virgin

> To show thro' th' darkness, descending,
> A cheerier way to die (p 177),

a plea which will form its own ironic commentary in the context of the play as a whole.

The description of the 'miraculous' return of the transfigured statue, seen in a 'vision' by little Ursula and one of the men, is also meant to be strongly ironic: 'From her window, little Ursula looked, and saw Her come in; in th' moonlight, along the street She came, stately. Blinded by the coloured light that shone around about Her, the child fell back, in a swoon she fell full on the floor beneath her' (p 177). Since we know that the 'miracle' has been wrought by trickery, it is clear that the people are deceiving themselves, for they desperately need to believe that their lives, too, can be transformed by colour and beauty. Thus the vision, like the transformation itself, is a false one, clinging stubbornly to its ironic context and unable to transmute it. On the realistic surface of the action, then, both 'miracle' and 'vision' – like the regal beauty of colour in 'play' and song that momentarily adorns the dreary tenement – prefigure the truly miraculous vision which occurs in Act iii. Yet what the expressionism of *Red Roses* reveals is the ironic undersurface which explores the difference between a false transformation that cannot change the lives of the people in any meaningful way, and the true transformation which Dublin and her people undergo in the last half of the play.

In *The Silver Tassie*, the search for the absent soldier in the expressionist Act ii led to the discovery of some startling transformations, as well as to the discovery of the complex organic unity which underlies the play as a whole. In *Red Roses for Me*, similar discoveries occur in the expressionist Act iii, where – though the plaster statue has disappeared – Our Lady of Eblana, herself, reappears in many forms in the expressionism of the second half of the play. And when she does reappear she speaks of ideals which are no longer remote and illusory, but which are in the process of becoming an essential and meaningful part of the lives of the Dublin poor.

THE BRIDGE OF VISION

The visionary third act of *Red Roses for Me* is the heart and soul of O'Casey's drama, the timeless arena in which the central action of the play takes place. Intermingling images of light and darkness, realized visibly onstage by the lighting technician, continue to speak vividly of a world of light struggling to emerge out of the darkness of the Dublin slums. This conflict is realized, too, by a number of confrontations which will begin to answer those insistent questions, raised in the previous acts, concerning the plight of the Dublin poor. The struggle which ensues in the last half of the play, however, is not merely a corporeal one, but one which shows the consciousness of the people gradually awakening, from gloom and despair, to joy and faith, as they cast off the false ideals which have been imprisoning them.

For the first time in the play, the stage setting is out-of-doors, yet there is no immediate sense of relief from the dreary and crowded interior of the tenement. Though the scene takes place at the bridge which Ayamonn has earlier referred to as 'the bridge of vision' (p 153), the 'black an' bitther' (p 191) waters of the River Liffey only mirror the shadowy darkness that seems to be the inevitable lot of the Dublin poor. The men lounging on the parapets of the bridge are recognizably those 'in the previous scenes' (p 185) who accompanied, in ritual procession, the statue of Our Lady of Eblana. Yet their prayer to the statue, 'lift up th' poor heads ever bending,' (p 177) has clearly gone unanswered, for 'their expressionless faces [are] hidden by being bent down towards their breasts' (p 185).

Sitting in the more immediate foreground, Eeada, Dympna, and Finnoola appear as caricatures of the Three Fates spinning the thread which makes up the torn and tangled fabric of Ireland. Once more they attempt to direct the course of the action and improve in some way the tangled course of their lives. 'Dressed so in black that they appear to be enveloped in the blackness of a dark night' (pp 185–6), the three women are trying to earn a few shillings by peddling cakes, apples, and flowers on the Dublin streets. Despite the restoration of the statue of Our Lady of Eblana, the women have been overcome by weariness and a sense of futility. Nor is there anything to counteract the diabolic vision of Dublin as 'A graveyard where th' dead are all above th' ground,' which now sweeps suddenly across the stage: 'This spongy leaden sky's Dublin; those tomby houses is Dublin too – Dublin's scurvy body; an' we're Dublin's silver soul. (*She spits vigorously into the street.*) An' that's what Eeada thinks of th' city's soul an' body!' (p 186).

The drowsiness of the three women, and the monotonous 'sing-song' voice in which they speak, suggests, on the level of the play's expressionism, the trance-like state of the oracle. In this manner, Eeada's words rise, as if from out of the unconscious, and are linked, by their imagery, to the two most dominant forces at work in present-day Ireland. Though Eeada is not fully aware of it, what her words imply is an instinctive rejection of these powers, for the ideals which Church and State should embody have grown meaningless in the bitter context of their lives.

As is usual with O'Casey, the stage setting is used deliberately and effectively to make concrete and real what might otherwise tend towards the abstract:

> *In the distance, where the street, leading from the bridge, ends in a point of space, to the right, soars the tapering silver spire of a church; and to the left, Nelson's Pillar, a deep red, pierces the sky, with Nelson, a deep black, on its top, looking over everything that goes on around him.* (p 185)

The dominance of both Church and State, then, are made evident by the stage setting from the time the curtain rises. Ironically, however, the 'silver spire,' symbolic of the Church (both Catholic and Protestant), is far off in the distance, remote from the people who, Eeada says, are 'Dublin's silver soul.' In this way, the silver spire is like the statue of the first half of the play, apparently a source of comfort and strength yet unable to help the people. Similarly, Nelson, atop his red pillar, is one of the 'great men' whose greatness Eeada calls into question, along with the greatness of Dublin herself. As a symbol of the glory and power of the State, Nelson's Pillar represents a force used to subjugate the people, rather than a source of protection and help.[15]

An awareness of what Ireland has lost also struggles to the forefront of Finnoola's consciousness as she, too, begins to awaken from the 'nightmare' of Irish history: 'A gold-speckled candle, white as snow, was Dublin once; yellowish now, leanin' sideways, an' guttherin' down to a last shaky glimmer in th' wind o' life' (p 187). In the context of the informing imagery of the play as a whole, Finnoola's words should recall the religious ritual of the first two acts, the procession with the statue of the Virgin, and 'th' tall candles wait[ing] to be lit' (p 163) at the deathbed of

Mrs Breydon's Catholic neighbour. Though the plaster statue is no longer present onstage, 'Our Lady of Eblana' is whispered about in the imagery of Finnoola's words in a way which recalls, not the statue's new 'false' glory, but its fall from the original splendour it once had. Thus, in preparation for the awakening of the people to the beatific vision of Dublin as the City of God which forms the climax of the play, the movement of the first part of Act III is upward: from the nightmarish vision of a ghost city of living dead, to the barest stirrings of an awakened consciousness, which, in recalling the splendour of Ireland's glorious past, evokes a dim awareness of the need for a prophet who can restore something of that past glory to her people.

Until that time arrives, however, Eeada's bitter words suggest that only the ironic remnants of the spirit of the past remain alive in the present: 'Well, we've got Guinness's Brewery still, givin' us a needy glimpse of a betther life an hour or so on a Saturday night, though I hold me hand at praisin' th' puttin' of Brian Boru's golden harp on every black porther bottle' (p 187). Brian Boru, one of the mightiest of Ireland's kings, gave his life, almost a thousand years ago, to free Ireland from the domination of the Danes. Yet it is not very likely that this kind of bottled 'spirit' will be able to inspire the valorous deeds still needed to further the cause of Ireland's freedom. In fact, it is because past ideals remain so remote and illusory that the people are unable to comprehend their fate, though they stand on the bridge of vision – that bridge which links past, present, and future.

Across this bridge now comes the first of a number of figures, each of whom embodies in the present, however imperfectly, past ideals which had once been a vital part of Ireland's life. The Rector, Mr Clinton, who plays a political role by encouraging the strikers, and Inspector Finglas, a member of the mounted police and the Rector's churchwarden, are the modern-day incarnations of Church and State. These two figures – one all in black, one with a silver spike on his helmet – have appeared in the distance, as if from out of the past, as if having just stepped down from the lofty eminence of pillar and spire. The splendour of their dress, however, suggests a certain remoteness from the lives of the people, a distancing which should be confirmed by their positioning on the bridge above the heads of the despondent Dubliners. As the ensuing action makes plain, the Rector embodies the powers of both Church and State when used with some degree of insight and humanity. In this respect he provides a sharp contrast to Inspector Finglas, whose use of these powers is not just inhumane, but, by the end of the play, seems almost diabolical. Their opposing roles are further suggested by their contrasting dress and linked, as well, to that conflict which is central to the play: a world of light and colour, set in opposition to a world of darkness, and the struggle to belong to the one, rather than to the other. Here, O'Casey continues his symbolic use of colour and costuming.

The 'immaculate black' (p 188) suit, together with the 'vivid green scarf' (p 180) that the Rector wears, suggests not only his role as a minister of the Church in which he must confront the powers of darkness, but also the life-and-death struggle which he will support against these dark powers. Ironically, then, his dress links him to that other prominent black-clad figure onstage – the one atop the red pillar whose might has dominated Ireland and her people for centuries. There is no green about the statue, however, for that colour is also symbolic of the national identity of Ireland, which, when reborn, must be transfigured, as it is in the broad humanity of the Rector, to include Protestant and Catholic alike. Similarly, the silver accents on the Inspector's uniform, his sword and crown and especially the long silver spike on his helmet, link him visually with the silver spire in the distance and are clearly meant to reinforce the association between the oppressive might of Church and State which the Rector opposes. In this context, the crimson plume which 'flows' from the silver spike anticipates, as does the red pillar, the blood of sacrifice which will be shed, when, in Act IV, the police and the strikers clash.

The lack of insight which underlies the churchwarden's inhumanity is emphasized by the fact that he sees the poor, not as people, but as things – 'flotsam and jetsam'[16] – and his encounter with the reality of their world provokes an outburst of fury which is out of all proportion to the event. The Inspector's invective draws on images from an animal world and is as much a reflection of the nature of the speaker as it is of the debased condition of the Dublin poor, an irony which is echoed by rhythms and idioms which are alike in the speech of both:

INSPECTOR (*springing back with an angry exclamation*) What th' hell are you after doing, you rotten lizard! Looka what you've done, you mangy rat!
(*He takes hold of the lounger and shakes him sharply.*)
2ND MAN (*sleepily resentful*) Eh, there! Wha' th' hell?
INSPECTOR (*furiously*) You spat on my boots, you tousled toad – my boots, boots, boots!
2ND MAN (*frightened and bewildered*) Boots, sir? Is it me, sir? Not me, sir. Musta been someone else, sir. (p 190)

The Rector's confrontation with the people, on the other hand, is both sympathetic and humane, though he apparently does not recognize them as the same men and women he passed among at the entrance to the Breydon home. Nor does he speak directly to them. This failure of recognition and inability to communicate is itself symptomatic of the failure of either Church or State to do anything about the life of grinding poverty led by the poor, and is dramatized now by the way in which the Rector flings the woman a shilling, 'two tiny sixpences – fourpence a head' (p 191), an amount which is simply not enough. There is irony as well as pathos in the fear and sadness the Rector feels as he is aware of turning away from 'these sad things' who may yet have within them 'the Kingdom of Heaven' (p 191). Here, the Rector's words are based on scriptural authority[17] and serve to anticipate the awakening of that inner kingdom in the vision of Dublin as the City of God.

In the meantime, however, the intrusion of the Rector and Inspector Finglas have left the poor sunk almost as deeply in gloom as ever. Yet, in spite of their despair, the women's thoughts turn instinctively to memories of the brief joys of youth, memories which convey a sense of the splendour and richness of the past attempting to break through into the present:

EEADA (*mournfully*) ... Tormented with joy I was then as to whether I'd parade th' thronged sthreets on th' arm of a 16th Lancer, his black-breasted crimson coat a sight to see, an' a black plume droopin' from his haughty helmet; or lay claim to a red-breasted Prince o' Wales's Own, th' red plume in his hat a flame over his head.

DYMPNA It was a 15th King's Own Hussar for me, Eeada, with his rich blue coat an' its fairyland o' yellow braid, two yellow sthripes down his trousers, an' a red bag an' plume dancin' on his busby. (pp 191–2)

Onstage the bent heads and ragged dress of the 'loungers' provide an ironic contrast to the imaginary parade of the uniformed soldiers that spring to life in the women's vivid description. Paradoxically, there is a strong suggestion that the present can either be imprisoned by the past, or else liberated by it. For, while its colour and vitality still seem illusory to the Dublin poor, there is just a hint that their patched coats, too, like those of the Irish rebel Finnoola describes, are 'threaded with th' colours from the garment of Finn Mac Cool' (p 192). Thus, if the 'expressionless' faces and huddled postures of the men still speak of their imprisonment, the faded colours of their patched clothing now whisper of the barest possibility of freedom.

And yet it arouses painful and ambivalent emotions to be awakened to the grim reality of the present from dreams of a golden past or an even more golden future. Since Brennan does inadvertently awaken them, as he, in turn, crosses the bridge of vision to confront the people, their reaction is understandably one of bitterness. Nor is this the first time Brennan has encountered their hostility; and now, as he did when he took the statue to regild it, he braves their anger to present them with a vision of loveliness. His song is about young love in the springtime, the very thing the women have been dreaming about, and it is ironic that Eeada and Dympna cannot see themselves in the song. For the ecstasy of the young lovers actually looks forward to that ecstatic moment where Ayamonn and Finnoola meet, to dance together on the bridge of vision in a world which has been transfigured to beauty and joy.

Until now, the movement of the act, which has been trying to struggle upward out of an abyss of despair, has been given momentum by a series of confrontations, each of which suggests a possible source of hope only to have it prove false. However, with the entrance of Roory, the people are confronted, for the first time, with the possibility of realizing the ideals of the past in the present, of making their dreams of joy and freedom a reality. Roory partly understands why Brennan's song has failed to inspire the people, since he is able to recognize that what imprisons the poor is their own fear. The songs he would have Brennan sing, then, are ones which would inspire courage by the telling of valorous deeds:

Pearl of th' White Breasts, now, or Battle Song o' Munster that would pour into yous Conn's battle-fire of th' hundhred fights ... Leadher of Magh Femon's Host he was, Guardian of Moinmoy, an' Vetheran of our river Liffey, flowin' through a city whose dhrinkin' goblets once were made of gold, ere wise men carried it with frankincense an' myrrh to star-lit Bethlehem. (p 195)

Here, Roory's invocation of the fighting spirit of the pagan warriors of the past mingles oddly with the invocation of the spirit embodied in the birth of the 'Prince of Peace.' At the same time, the reintroduction of the motif of 'saviour' awakens the momentary hope that Roory – if not Brennan – will be able to find 'a song all men can sing' (p 169). Yet the people are unable to see themselves as part of the brave world that he envisions, and so reject Roory more in sadness than in anger.

Ayamonn, who has accompanied Roory on to the bridge of vision, now tries courageously to interrupt the dark reverie of the poor in words which seem at once preposterous and enigmatic: 'Rouse yourselves; we hold a city in our hands!' (p 196). Nor is he daunted by their bitter choral-like response, but, with vigorous and realistic words, breaks through their ritualizing of pain in which the demonic vision of Dublin that began the act floods with renewed intensity on to the stage:

FINNOOLA ... It's a bleak, black, an' bitther city.
1ST MAN Like a batthered, tatthered whore, bullied by too long a life.
2ND MAN An' her three gates are castles of poverty, penance, an' pain.
AYAMONN She's what our hands have made her. We pray too much and work too little. Meanness, spite, and common pattherns are woven thick through all her glory; but her glory's there for open eyes to see. (p 196)

In the context of the play's expressionism, Ayamonn's words should recall, not only the stooped, despairing figures that filled the stage as the act began, but also the sombre, ritualized procession of the first half of the play in which the Dublin poor carried the plaster statue of Our Lady of Eblana.

The people see in Ayamonn a person who is sympathetic to their plight and whose vision they can trust, one who 'knows things hid from us' (p 196). Immediately, they think of Mrs Breydon and her many kindnesses, and, in Finnoola's description of her, the 'glory' which Ayamonn has told them can be discerned in 'common pattherns' at once becomes a reality:

For all her tired look an' wrinkled face, a pure white candle she is, blessed this minute by St Colmkille of th' gentle manner, or be Aidan, steeped in th' lore o' heaven, or be Lausereena of th' silver voice an' snowy vestments—th' blue cloak o' Brigid be a banner over her head for ever! (p 197)

Without being fully aware of the import of their words, the Catholic women speak of the Protestant Mrs Breydon as an incarnation of the help they needed but did not get from the newly regilded, though quite lifeless, statue of Our Lady of Eblana. As in Acts I and II, the candle imagery, together with the imagery of colour and costuming, links the Madonna figure with the figure of Kaithleen ni Houlihan, both of whom merge in Mrs Breydon, herself, to suggest the reality of a united Ireland.

That such an Ireland can actually be found within the hearts of the poor people of Dublin is an idea which Roory cannot grasp, and, ironically, his concept of liberating Ireland does not include them:

ROORY (*hotly*) An' d'ye think talkin' to these tatthered second-hand ghosts'll bring back Heaven's grace an' Heaven's beauty to Kaithleen ni Houlihan?
AYAMONN Roory, Roory, your Kaithleen ni Houlihan has th' bent back of an oul' woman as well as th' walk of a queen. We love th' ideal Kaithleen ni Houlihan, not because she is false, but because she is beautiful; we hate th' real Kaithleen ni Houlihan, not because she is true, but because she is ugly.
(p 197)

Clearly, the impatient and zealous Roory cannot understand, and, as he hurries off angrily from the bridge of vision, it becomes apparent that O'Casey is dismissing the kind of rabid, 'single-vision' type of nationalist which Roory represents. However, Roory has helped to define, as did Brennan, those qualities that are necessary to save Ireland.

And Ayamonn possesses these qualities in abundance, for he has, not only vision, courage, and compassion, but also the ability to move people to action through the power of the spoken word. He understands the power of a word to awaken the spirit of man, whether it is the word of God, spoken out of the darkness at the dawn of creation 'when th' spirit of God first moved on th' face of th' waters' (p 197); or whether it is the word of Shakespeare, who is 'part of the kingdom of heaven in the nature of everyman' (p 131); or whether it is the word of the minstrel or of the political orator. The parallel between Ayamonn and O'Casey himself is now at its strongest, for the play is a striking testament to the power of the word as wielded by the creative imagination.

Rather than speaking of a far-off past or a far-off future, Ayamonn suggests the possibility of both past and future becoming part of a fulfilled present, a time that is 'precious here' (pp 195–6). He speaks of the need for action, telling the people to forget Roory 'an' remember ourselves, and think of what we can do to pull down th' banner from dusty bygones, an' fix it up in th' needs an' desires of today' (pp 197–8). Yet neither his words, nor his earlier entrance, has been accompanied by any general brightening of the stage. Instead, the growing darkness which is the visible metaphor for the gloom and despair which is stifling Dublin and her poor intensifies until 'things are but dimly seen, save the silver spire and the crimson pillar in the distance; and Ayamonn's head set in a streak of sunlight, looking like the severed head of Dunn-Bo speaking out of the darkness' (p 198).

The foreshadowing of Ayamonn's death which is implicit here does not, of course, depend upon the audience being able to recall the legend of Dunn-Bo – a minstrel-warrior who fought by the side of the king of Erin and whose head, set on a pillar, sang after death – but merely upon the lighting technician's ability to realize the effect of a 'severed head,' itself an image of sacrifice. Nor does the effect of the catalogue of the names and deeds of Irish kings and heroes depend on a knowledge of Irish history and folklore. All that is necessary is that we recognize the invocation of a past made golden by the heroism and sacrifice of Celtic warriors, a past which we now foresee will live again in the heroic deeds and sacrificial death of Ayamonn. There is a note of prophecy, then, as the severed head begins to speak, though at the same time the words themselves create an unexpected effect, for they cannot at first escape the hollow, rhetorical ring of the enthusiastic, but inexperienced, young orator who declaims them: 'Our sthrike is yours. A step ahead for us today; another one for you tomorrow. We who have known, and know, the emptiness of life shall know its fullness' (p 198).

This unusual scene – realized so suddenly onstage – is both grotesque and sublime. Its grotesqueness speaks of the horror and obscenity of death in the coming sacrifice; its sublimity speaks movingly of man's heroic endeavours which seem all the more heroic because they defy our sense of the absurd. This quality about O'Casey's work, though at all times uniquely his own, links him, not only to Expressionist theatre, but also, at least as closely, to the Theatre of the Absurd.

The physical elevation of Ayamonn to the level of silver spire and crimson pillar – realized onstage by the effect of lighting and by his position on the upper part of the bridge – also suggests his new role of authority in the lives of the people, an authority based on a sense of the rightful heritage belonging to the poor of Dublin. Though at first the women reject his words because they fear the violence of the coming struggle, Ayamonn is finally able to sweep away their fears even as his words seem, miraculously, to dispel the darkness. As the setting sun floods the scene with golden, bronze, and coloured light, Ayamonn's words grow luminous with the natural beauty of the scene before him:

Don't flinch in th' first flare of a fight ... Take heart of grace from your city's hidden splendour ... Oh, look! Look there! Th' sky has thrown a gleaming green mantle over her bare shoulders, bordhered with crimson, an' with a hood of gentle magenta over her handsome head – look!
(*The scene has brightened, and bright and lovely colours are being brought to them by the caress of the setting sun. The houses on the far side of the river now bow to the visible world, decked in mauve and burnished bronze; and the men that have been lounging against them now stand stalwart, looking like fine bronze statues, slashed with scarlet ...*)
Look! Th' vans an' lorries rattling down th' quays, turned to bronze an' purple by th' sun, look like chariots forging forward to th' battle-front. (pp 198–9)

Here, then, is the true miracle: the beauty of the natural world illuminating, and made luminous by, the heart, and the mind, of man. Coloured by what may seem to be a divinely inspired nature and shaped by the human imagination, a gentle madonna figure appears and merges with the beautiful Kathleen ni Houlihan to form a truly Irish madonna, one who wears 'a gleaming green mantle over her bare shoulders, bordhered with crimson an' ... a hood of gentle magenta over her handsome head,' one who is, as Eeada realizes, 'Shy an' lovely, as well as battle-minded!' Unlike the plaster statue of Our Lady of Eblana, or the Kathleen ni Houlihan described by Ayamonn earlier, this Kathleen, like the one in Ayamonn's song, is both true and beautiful.

But if Ayamonn's words have evoked another genesis, it is one which anticipates from its beginning the sacrifice which is, paradoxically, its very life. The emphasis of the scene as a whole, however, is away from this dark element of sacrifice and towards a joyous celebration of new life and strength. At first, the rays of the dying sun, struggling to break through the 'gloomy, grey sky' (p 185) touch only the houses and people 'on the far side of the river' (p 199); then the light sweeps across the bridge on to the forefront of the stage so that the transformation, not only of the city, but of the poor people themselves, is immediate and breathtaking. Suddenly the actors and the stage itself are transformed as the imagery of the spoken word is caught up and realized in the visible imagery of lighting and costuming. The bleak, expressionless faces of the men and women who carried, in a joyless procession, the lifeless statute of Our Lady of Eblana have all vanished. Instead, the stage is filled with 'sturdy men of bronze,' whose faces, 'like the women's,' are 'aglow' with the courageous spirit of the heroic warriors of the past.[18] These are the living 'statues' that suggest, not a lifeless and dead ideal, but a people in whose hearts have been emblazoned the miraculous vision they have just witnessed. Thus the final transfiguration of Our Lady of Eblana reveals her to be a living, redemptive force at the heart of both city and people.

As the women rise upward into the light, a sense of ecstasy sweeps irresistibly over the stage to find its expression, quite spontaneously, in the jubilation of song and dance. Each of the women has 'a sober black shawl hide ... her body entirely,' until, as she is transformed by her vision, the shawl slips away to reveal hues of dark or lighter green mingled with silver. The joyous song and the dance of life that grip Finnoola and Ayamonn proclaim a time when the Kathleens of Ireland are no longer 'of the Sorrows,'[19] and, for the moment at least, the proclamation is believed.

The extremely complex way in which O'Casey has used colour and costumes for symbolic purposes – and so integrated his 'stage magic' into the dramatic structure of the play as a whole – now becomes ever more apparent. Earlier in the play, the colourful costumes of royalty put on over everyday clothing symbolized a false nobility, a false transfiguration imposed from without, like the gilding on the statue of Our Lady of Eblana. Whereas here, when the black shawls which make the women a part of the world of darkness are finally cast off, what is revealed by their colourful silver and green dress is that they are now a part of that world of light and colour for which they have so longed. And what this effect, in turn, suggests is that a true transformation must come from within the hearts and minds of the people themselves.

As if to confirm this fact, towards the end of the transformation scene, the 'labour' song which springs spontaneously to Ayamonn's lips is immediately caught up and sung by the Dublin poor, for Ayamonn has truly inspired the people by opening their eyes to a beauty which they had almost forgotten ever existed. The men, though still weary, are quite different from the men we saw 'lounging' about the stage at the opening curtain. Now they are quick to recognize – and to oppose – the dissonant note that threatens the joyous harmony of their song:

> 1ST MAN (*gloomily, but with a note of defiance in his voice*) Th' thramp of marchin' soldiers out to prevent our meetin' an' to stop our sthrike.
> 2ND MAN (*in a burst of resolution*) We'll have both, in spite of them! (p 203)

This newly awakened determination of the men to fight for the ideal of a truly liberated Ireland is the final dramatic testimony to the fact that the ideal is more than illusion: it is backed by living men of flesh and blood. The bronze statues, symbolic of the heroic spirit of Ireland's glorious past, have sprung to life – they are a bit dazed perhaps from their long sleep, but they are ready to answer the challenge to battle.

THE ARTIST'S ROLE: LAMPLIGHTER OF THE IMAGINATION

The puzzling disappearance of the plaster statue from the structure of *Red Rose for Me* was resolved on the bridge of vision by the miraculous return of Our Lady of Eblana in a variety of transfigured 'images.' These images speak of ideals which, as they are awakened within the human heart and mind, are capable of being translated into the world around us. In Act IV, the part the creative imagination can fulfil in such an awakening to action is demonstrated by Ayamonn, whose visionary role, as he discovers, has nothing to do with ivory towers, or with tenement doors fast shut. Instead, while struggling to realize the ideal world of his song, Ayamonn has found himself caught up in the lives of the Dublin poor and in the conflict which is an inescapable part of the world around us.

Although we will see nothing of the actual clash between the strikers and the forces of law and order who oppose them, Eeada's graphic, eyewitness account and Finnoola's dramatic entrance, pale and faint from the injury she has received, realize enough of the suffering that has been caused to prepare for the one death which informs the concluding action of the play. That death is, inevitably, Ayamonn's though the Inspector, in his attempt to blunt the effect of Ayamonn's loss and so win over Sheila, tries to make himself appear blameless, and the death, an unfortunate accident: 'Believe me, I did my best. I thought the charge would send them flying, but they wouldn't budge; wouldn't budge, till the soldiers fired, and he was hit. Believe me, I did my best. I tried to force my horse between them and him' (p 225). At first Sheila believes what the Inspector is saying, though this viewing of Ayamonn's death is one which effectively robs it of all meaning. A cosmos ruled by chance, an accidental cosmos, is one in which chaos is come again, but even chaos is preferable to another martyrdom which cannot be countenanced by the authorities. To steal away their 'saviour' is, in fact, the final theft that this most militant representative of Church and State will attempt to perpetrate on the defenceless Dublin poor.

Thus, as the Inspector tries to steal away the love which Sheila feels for the memory of Ayamonn, his actions, if successful, would also have the effect of belittling Ayamonn in the eyes of the very men and women who had followed him into battle. O'Casey's stage directions make plain that something which will affect the fate of the poor Dubliners is about to occur: the Inspector and Sheila 'have walked to the gateway, and now stand there together, the men and women along the hedge eyeing them, though pretending to take no notice' (p 226). As in the first half of the play, individual actions continue to take on symbolic dimensions as they occur against a background of suffering humanity, represented stylistically by the choral grouping of Dublin poor.

Ironically, as the Inspector tries to shape Sheila's viewing of what has occurred, all that happens is that she is reminded – no doubt by the Inspector's exaggerated poetic language – of Ayamonn's vision of her as the black-shawled Kathleen of the Red Roses. In the bitter context of the lovers' quarrel which divided them, a motif which, together with the motif of theft, is echoed here for the last time, Sheila recalls Ayamonn's final challenge: 'He said that roses red were never meant for me' (p 226). Yet, moments earlier, Sheila has been carrying red roses, placing them on Ayamonn's breast as his body is carried into the church. Her acknowledgement of the role which she has previously rejected is thus movingly enacted onstage, while her sorrowing words, 'Ayamonn, Ayamonn, my own poor Ayamonn' (p 224), are an implicit recognition of the sacrifice which has been made in order for Ayamonn's vision to become a reality. Here, Sheila's keening of her lover's name – *Ay-a-monn* – becomes the eloquent cry of a humanity whose nature is inextricably linked to suffering, but whose godhead is undeniably affirmed in 'th' echo of [its] own shout' (p 179).[20] Sheila's sudden angry denunciation of the Inspector – 'Oh, you dusky-minded killer of more worthy men!' (p 226) – rises out of that moment of illumination which has allowed her to become, at last, the Kathleen of Ayamonn's song.

Throughout the play, however, O'Casey has been careful to do more than merely caricature the Inspector as the 'villain' of the piece, for to do so would allow us to underestimate the very real power such a person is able to wield. Quite unlike Foster and Dowzard (each of whom, like Rosencrantz and Guildenstern, would exist only in one dimension were it not for the fact that there are two of them), the Inspector manages to appear quite human at times – and, at such times, is most dangerous. On the other hand, though he does not appear in the first two acts, the strong force of his presence is felt, for he has been able to manipulate the Rector and Sheila, and, through them, has very nearly been able to manipulate Ayamonn. But now the Inspector's role of diabolic artisan is clearly revealed and he condemns himself by his own angry words. His savage dismissal of the Dublin poor, whom he despises all the more since they have just witnessed his defeat, recalls the extremely inhumane attitude both to the poor and to Ayamonn which he revealed in Act III. In the last half of the play the Rector consistently opposes the Inspector's view, as, in words which specifically invoke the religious symbolism of the play, he states with a quiet conviction that viewing of Ayamonn which Act IV confirms: 'Ayamonn Breydon has within him the Kingdom of Heaven' (p 191).

If Inspector Finglas' really Satanic role of the guileful tempter – first of Ayamonn, then of Sheila – is misinterpreted, and if his sometimes apparently sympathetic words are taken to be kind and helpful advice, then the dramatic relevance of Sheila's vacillating behaviour is lost and she can appear, quite wrongly, as 'small and mean against the grandeur of

Ayamonn's ideals and sacrifice.'[21] Moreover, the significance of her decision to look at Ayamonn's death, not as the Inspector would have her view it, but as Ayamonn himself would see it, cannot be understood:

> INSPECTOR (*from where he is near the tree*) It wasn't a very noble thing to die for a single shilling.
> SHEILA Maybe he saw the shilling in th' shape of a new world. (p 225)

Here we must recognize the symbolic role of the Inspector – which is confirmed stylistically, as his words grown ever more sibilant, by his positioning, Judas-like, near the tree – since, without a sense of the 'worth' of the antagonist, the sacred nature of Ayamonn's struggle, which will continue even after his death, is much diminished. Thus, while the curtain fall that divides the act signals the end of Ayamonn's performance on the stage of life, the curtain rising, as the play continues, suggests his never-ending role in the struggle against the powers of darkness.

Indeed, from the beginning of the act, the stylized churchyard setting makes plain that the Christ-like pattern which has been weaving its way into Ayamonn's life cannot be prevented. The motif of sacrifice is embodied in the 'yellow robe of St Peter and the purple robe of St Paul' (p 222), martyred saints whose lives are depicted in the stained glass window of the church – a window which now replaces onstage the one in the Breydon home with its 'cross' and 'altar' of flowers.[22] In addition, the colours of the beautiful geranium and musk and fuchsia are picked up once again in the symbolic colours of Easter evident in the churchyard, even as these same colours – the crimson, gold, and purple of the setting sun – have transfigured the city of Dublin in the visionary Act III.

The highly formal structure of this concluding act is seen, too, in the fact that it is the only one to begin, as well as end, with a song. The hymn which the Rector is singing as the curtain rises associates the miracle of the resurrection with the no less miraculous courage of 'every man' (Ay-a-monn) who defies death in order to oppose 'Th' power bestow'd on fool or knave' (p 206). The farcical scene which follows makes clear that the reference is to Foster and Dowzard, the two 'Select' vestrymen of St Burnupus, who object to the cross of daffodils made by Ayamonn and demand to have it removed from the church, for their single vision sees it only as a 'Popish emblem' (p 208), despite the fact that it has 'a Keltic shape' (p 219).

It is through this farcical charge of 'Popery,' brought against both the Rector and Ayamonn, that O'Casey reveals the false ideals – the 'sham' –

which dominate the Christian community and prevent a true spirit of brotherhood and communion among all men. And, as Mrs Breydon points out in the following scene, in words which are a realistic appraisal of the danger Ayamonn will have to face: 'Shams are powerful things, mustherin' at their broad backs guns that shoot, big jails that hide their foes, and high gallows to choke th' young cryin' out against them when th' stones are silent' (pp 209–10). Sheila's words also add to our sense of foreboding as she pleads with the Rector to 'let this power go on its way of darkened grandeur, and let Ayamonn sit safe by his own fireside' (p 210). Significantly, it is just at this moment that the Inspector, 'in full uniform,' appears from one direction, while Ayamonn, followed by the men and women he will lead into battle appears from the opposite direction.

The tableau scene which follows, where the men and women in chorus claim Ayamonn as their own against all those forces which would hold him back, is a return to the more overt expressionism of the play, and to that expressionist technique first used at the end of Act I of *The Silver Tassie*. Once more, the stage directions make clear O'Casey's meaning:

> *The men and women spread along the path outside, and stay still watching those in the grounds from over the hedge. They hold themselves erect, now; their faces are still pale, but are set with seams of resolution. Each is wearing in the bosom a golden-rayed sun.*
> (p 210)

The symbolic sun[23] recalls the transformation scene of Act III and so confirms that the strength needed to effect the transfiguration of Dublin and her people resides in the hearts of the men and women before us.

Symbolically, at all times throughout the act, the chorus of men and women move and stand outside the iron railing which, though it is almost hidden by the green and golden hedge, nevertheless effectively bars them from the garden and keeps them a part of the 'poor and smoky district' (p 205) behind them. Ayamonn's obvious haste – 'I come but to go' (p 210) – and the few words he takes time to speak, each charged with urgency, already distances him from those in the garden even during the few moments he is in it. Indeed, his continued and deliberate absence from the garden sanctuary seems, itself, a presentiment of his death. Ayamonn's last speech before his leave-taking consists of only four words, 'I go with you!' (p 211). Paradoxically, they seem characterless and, as they echo the words of the chorus, 'He comes with us!' they seem devoid of all will. Yet his words are an expression of a more universal will, one which goes beyond the merely personal to become truly selfless in its dedication to humanity. Again, there is a sense of Ayamonn's elevation to an almost god-like role. The expressionsim here is as far from the realistic technique as it was in the Dunn-Bo scene. And the effect, which O'Casey seems to aim at quite consciously, is to heighten our awareness of the universal morality-type figures who masquerade in the everyday dress of apparently realistic characters in a drama which is already a modern miracle play and which will become, before the act is over, a modern passion play.

Certainly, it is growing more and more obvious that the dark powers that will oppose Ayamonn are not merely the forces of law and order. The Inspector makes it quite plain that the Authorities set themselves above the law: 'Remember, all! When swords are drawn and horses charge, the kindly Law, so fat with hesitation, swoons away, and sees not, hears not, cares not what may happen' (p 212). Clearly, the true nature of the power the Inspector is intent on evoking exceeds even the rightful extent of the Church and State he represents. Mrs Breydon has no difficulty in understanding the Inspector's words, and when she does she is quick to realign her sympathies. Courageously, despite her fears, Mrs Breydon now sends Ayamonn off with her blessing to fight against the 'sham' world that the Inspector embodies. Though this is the last we see of Ayamonn, it is against the broad perspective afforded us by Ayamonn's humanity, that we continue to hear the splintered and fragmented opinions of those whose divided humanities could not, together, make up a 'whole man.'[24]

The pattern of action which now develops, as the motif of quarrelling crescendoes in violent conflict, is similar, in some respects, to that of the first half of the play. In fact, the fight between the strikers and the two 'scabs,' Foster and Dowzard, results, like the earlier eruption of violence in Act II, in some arrant cowards desperately seeking shelter from a stone-throwing mob. The parallelism points to a use of character which is expressionist and explains why Roory and Mullcanny do not appear in Act IV: their remaining dramatic and symbolic function has been taken over by Foster and Dowzard. Here, as in the earlier act, the violence which is a growing prelude to Ayamonn's death occurs offstage so that the focus is not on the skirmish itself, but on the kind of bigoted attitudes which lead to the struggle that follows. The scenes are farcical, but what they point to is tragic: man's inability to see who the real enemy is in a land so long divided by political and economic, as well as religious, conflict.

Appropriately, then, the focal point of conflict since the act began has been the 'living' cross of daffodils which Ayamonn has made. Like the earlier cross formed by the railway signal, it is a constant reminder of Ayamonn's role and the struggle for spiritual, as well as economic, freedom in which he is engaged. And the trampling of the cross of daffodils, which is the climax of Act IV and the resolution of the play, is the symbolic death of Ayamonn. O'Casey rewrote this scene to include a specific reference to Ayamonn and to introduce the offstage sound effects – 'a bugle-call sounding the charge,' the 'sound of galloping horses ... followed by several volleys of rifle-fire' (p 219) – all carefully timed to make clear, in retrospect, that Ayamonn's death by a soldier's bullet has coincided with Foster's and Dowzard's gleeful destruction of the beautiful cross of daffodils.[25]

Thus the symbolic setting of a sacrificial death confirms the parallel which has been suggested throughout the play between Ayamonn's life and the life of Christ, both of whom lived among the poor and among thieves, both of whom worked miracles in order to transform our way of viewing the world. Moreover, the crucifixion among thieves finds its parallel, too, in the ironic context in which Ayamonn's death takes place. Those who, like Eeada, have had their faith stolen away by fear, are ready to deny 'that mad fool, Breydon' (p 220), and the Inspector, as we have seen, is all too anxious to rob Ayamonn's death of any meaning.

Ayamonn's wish 'to lie in th' church tonight' (p 221) is carried out despite the opposition of Foster and Dowzard, and, with the entry of his lifeless body, 'a core o' darkness' (p 225), into the brightly lit church, there is a sense of the Church having entered once more into a meaningful role in the lives of the poeple. The Church is no longer a far-off silver spire as it was in Act III, nor is its presence symbolized now by a plaster statue unable to inspire and cheer those who look to it for comfort. Instead, life has flowed into the Church and around it; it has sheltered both Catholics and Protestants who have come to it in fear, and, finally, its spirit has been renewed by the act of faith and courage to which Ayamonn's death now bears mute testimony.

The new life which Ayamonn's death, like the death of every saint or martyr, has given to the Church is symbolized dramatically by the lights which are turned on again in the little church of St Burnupus, where Ayamonn's body lies. Then, as the darkness is dispelled in that moment before the final curtain falls, the discord of the play is at last resolved in harmony. It is Brennan who sings Ayamonn's lovely ballad, 'Red Roses for Me,' as 'a sign of respect an' affection; an' as a finisher-off to a last farewell' (p 227). But what we hear in the song is the voice of the warrior-minstrel Dunn-Bo telling of the miracle of yet another death and resurrection. And what we hear, too, is Ayamonn's own voice singing triumphantly from the bridge of vision beyond the grave.

Some eight years before writing *Red Roses for Me*, and six years after writing *The Silver Tassie*, O'Casey expressed the dramatic 'credo' which informs the visionary quality of his plays, especially as it is found in his two most visionary works:

The new form in drama will take qualities found in classical, romantic and expressionistic plays, will blend them together, breathe the breath of life into the new form and create a new drama. It will give rise to a new form of acting, a new form of production, a new response in the audience; author, actors and audience will be in communion with each other–three in one and one in three. If a play is what it ought to be it must be a religious function.[26]

Clearly, O'Casey's audacity as a playwright knew no bounds, and the challenge he poses the director is a formidable one.

It is a challenge, moreover, that can only be met when O'Casey's use of language is understood. At worst, his language falters badly, as, for example, when the Inspector calls Ayamonn 'a neat slab of a similar slime' (p 191). At best, his language, as well as being colourful, comic, and lyrical by turns, often creates imaginative patterns in which man is both juxtaposed against, and linked with, his universe. Ironically, a passage which has frequently been taken to discredit *Red Roses for Me* is actually one of the best examples of the kind of metaphysical–rather than simply rhetorical–structures that O'Casey delights in building. Ayamonn is addressing his mother, after she has saved Mullcanny from the rioters, as if she were (and is she not?) a person of great nobility. His words, once again, contain an odd echo of Shakespearean tragedy: 'Go an' lie down, lady; you're worn out. Time's a perjured jade, an' ever he moans a man must die' (p 179). The mistake in gender is far too obvious to be anything but deliberate on O'Casey's part and is meant to reveal the very human limitations of the 'romantic hero' at the exact moment when he is, all unknowingly, declaiming his own tragic destiny. That the destiny of every man can rise above the absurdity of circumstance to become noble and heroic is suggested by the simple eloquence with which Ayamonn describes man's aspirations:

Who through every inch of life weaves a patthern of vigour an' elation can never taste death, but goes to sleep among th' stars, his withered arms outstretched to greet th' echo of his own shout. It will be for them left behind to sigh for an hour, an' then to sing their own odd songs, an' do their own odd dances, to give a lonely God a little company, till they, too, pass by on their bare way out. When a true man dies, he is buried in th' birth of a thousand worlds. (p 179)

Here, juxtaposed in the very same passage with the absurd rhetoric of 'Time's a perjured jade,' O'Casey's imagery speaks movingly of crucifixion and resurrection; of despair transfigured to joy; of death, to victory–and of those who remain.

Prophet and visionary, dramatist and music hall comedian–O'Casey fuses many roles in writing *Red Roses for Me*, as he plays joyously with words and images, with symbols and techniques, making them perform tricks as dazzling as any circus-master: 'Hello, what kind of a circus is it's goin' on here?' (p 149), Roory asks; and Mullcanny demands: 'Is this a home-sweet-away-from-home hippodhrome, or what?' (p 151). As a rather enigmatic sign of his role as prophet, O'Casey wore the brightly coloured caps made first by his daughter, Shivaun, then later sent to him by people from all over the world, though the uncompromising honesty of the man reveals, even in his most visionary plays, that he could never fill this role in other than a mock-serious guise. Thus, in *Red Roses for Me*, the symbolic role in which we can see O'Casey is that of lamplighter.[27]

The curtain which, in Act IV, has fallen to mark the end of Ayamonn's performance on the stage of life, rises on a scene which is almost dark until it is illuminated by the 'little flower of light' (p 222) that the lamplighter carries:

LAMPLIGHTER What's up? What's on? What's happenin' here? What's they all doin' now?

1ST MAN Bringin' th' body o' Breydon to th' church.

LAMPLIGHTER Aw, is that it? Guessed somethin' was goin' on.

1ST MAN He died for us.

LAMPLIGHTER Looka that, now! An' they're all accouthered in their best to welcome him home, wha'? Aw, well, th' world's got to keep movin', so I must be off; so long! (pp 222–3)

The curiosity about life, the wonder of it, and the simple, homespun philosophy are all part of a man whose skilful dramatic craftsmanship allows him to illuminate scene after scene, in play after play, until somehow–miraculously–he illuminates both the heart and the mind of man.

4

A Revaluation in the Light of the Absurd

Sean O'Casey's response to the dark world of the absurdists was, quite simply, one of outrage. 'For the life of me,' he complained bitterly in 'The Bald Primaqueera,' the last article he wrote before his death, 'I can't find anything humanly absurd in any of them.'[1]

Earlier, in an article written especially for students of the theatre, he wrote indignantly:

Beckett? I have nothing to do with Beckett. He isn't in me; nor am I in him. I am not waiting for Godot to bring me life; I am out after life myself, even at the age I've reached. What have any of you to do with Godot? There is more life than Godot can give in the life of the least of us. That Beckett is a clever writer, and that he has written a rotting and remarkable play, there is no doubt; but his philosophy isn't my philosophy, for within him there is no hazard of hope; no desire for it; nothing in it but a lust for despair, and a crying of woe, not in a wilderness, but in a garden.[2]

Though there are many dark moments in O'Casey, certainly in the Dublin 'Tragedies,' what his most despairing play – The Silver Tassie – makes clear is that, however he might cry 'woe' in both garden and wilderness, the world, for him, was still a place of sacrament, a place which was at once both Eden and Gethsemane. Thus, as his own plays, culminating in Red Roses for Me and Cock-a-Doodle Dandy, grew more visionary and apocalyptic, he felt justified in protesting the bleak and pessimistic outlook of the younger generation of dramatists who were, to O'Casey's chagrin, obviously up-and-coming.

The sudden and almost inexplicable popularity which the new Theatre of the Absurd achieved during the last decade of O'Casey's lifetime must have perplexed him greatly. In view of his own failure to achieve the recognition that he felt his experimental plays deserved, and the more or less continuing eclipse of his own fortunes since the rejection of *The Silver Tassie*, the acceptance of even more wildly experimental plays in the popular and commercial theatres must have seemed totally unjust.

Indeed, we can gauge O'Casey's feeling here by comparing his final bitter lampooning of 'these Primaqueera playwrights' – Ionesco, Rudkin, Pinter – with his fierce praise of John Arden's anti-war play, *Serjeant Musgrave's Dance*. This play, with its structural use of music and song, its richly comic, brawling characters, and its brilliant climax in the grotesque scene of the hanging skeleton and the dance of death, is strikingly like O'Casey's own expressionist theatre. Nor could O'Casey have been unaware of the multiple ironies involved when he described Arden's work as

far and away the finest play of the present day, full of power, protest, and frantic compassion, notwithstanding that, on its first presentation, it was scowled and scooted from the theatre by most of our intelligent and unintelligent drama critics. I wonder why! What dazzling Freudian id or idiom swept this rejection into them, making them reject the denunciation of war's horrors, and led them to embrace the plays which despise and hate life.[3]

There is much restless energy – much wit and anger – in these two articles, one on Beckett's *Waiting for Godot*, the other on the Theatre of the Absurd and the Theatre of Cruelty, which, as O'Casey points out, go 'arm in arm.'[4] And this energy derives in part from the way in which he had himself been served, throughout his lifetime, by a host of reviewers and critics, all echoing the opinion of Yeats, who rejected *The Tassie* out of hand. O'Casey, while not entirely blameless in the matter, at least had the good sense to recognize what was involved: 'there goes a cursed opinion again,'[5] he told Yeats with a touch of self-mockery. And in the titles of his books, *The Flying Wasp* and *The Green Crow*, he acknowledges, with humour and courage and with a certain humility, the kind of pose vis-à-vis his detractors that he had been forced to adopt.

Despite the occasional error of fact or judgement, the value of O'Casey's own opinions on the Theatre of the Absurd lies in the energy, and even in the anger, with which they are expressed – an anger which is made palatable by wit, and an energy which remains vital and creative.

Thus, O'Casey's last written words intended for publication were not just a dismissal of what he felt to be the limited and one-sided vision of the absurdists, but also a strong affirmation of his own beliefs:

Ah, to hell with the loutish lust of Primaqueera. There are still many red threads of courage, many golden threads of nobility woven into the tingling fibres of our common humanity. No one passes through life scatheless. The world has many sour noises, the body is an open target for many invisible enemies, all hurtful, some venemous, like the accursed virus which can bite deeply into flesh and mind. It is full of disappointments, and too many of us have to suffer the loss of a beloved child, a wound that aches bitterly till our time here ends. Yet, even so, each of us, one time or another, can ride a white horse, can have rings on our fingers and bells on our toes, and, if we keep our senses open to the scents, sounds, and sights all around us, we shall have music wherever we go.[6]

The appeal to the child's world, to the 'authority' of the nursery rhyme, makes O'Casey's point with a characteristic and utterly convincing simplicity. Rhymes and songs, music and dance were all a part of that magical affirmation of life that O'Casey wanted to see on the contemporary stage, and the older he grew, the more magic became a part of his plays in the shape, for example, of a flying cock or a trumpeting statue. Thus – despite the *Tassie*'s rejection – O'Casey and Yeats were once more in agreement. In their later years, what they both tell us is that the proximity of death, the final cruelty in a cruel world, is not an occasion for even more metaphysical anguish at the absurdity of man's condition, but an occasion on which

Soul [must] clap its hands and sing, and louder sing
For every tatter in its mortal dress.[7]

It is, then, the optimistic belief that it is possible for man to transcend the absurdity of his condition which, above all, distinguishes an O'Casey play from the plays of Beckett and the Theatre of the Absurd, and from the plays of those other dramatists who have been influenced by Antonin Artaud's concept of the 'theatre of cruelty.'

Yet the difference is one of emphasis and degree, rather than one of absolute contrast, for O'Casey's world contains within it the world of the absurd – that often cruel world which each of us inhabits but which can at least be laughed at, if it cannot be dealt with in any other way. And it is this 'humanly absurd' aspect of O'Casey's theatre, embodied in the song and dance, the mask, mime, farce, and slapstick, the wild tragi-comic scenes in which the grotesque and the sublime mingle – in fact, all those elements which O'Casey uses to create his own kind of stage poetry – that allows us to view his plays as an unacknowledged seedbed from which grew many of the dramatic motifs and techniques of the Theatre of the Absurd. For when the curtain fell on the nearly empty stage of *Juno and the Paycock*, what the audience had glimpsed was the 'realistic' stage being stripped down to essentials in preparation for the curtain going up – a quarter century later – on the Theatre of the Absurd. Until recently, however, it has been O'Casey's own impassioned outcry against those 'Primaqueera' playwrights that has, to a large extent, obscured this fact.

THE STATE O' CHASSIS

Earlier, and in a more mellow mood, O'Casey had actually expressed a deep admiration for Beckett, even while recognizing the basic difference in their philosophies. In 'The Lark in the Clear Air Still Sings,' he wrote:

I was born to sing a different song, facing those singing the same song in many different keys – Kafka, Beckett, Ionesco, Greene, Eliot, Genêt, Orwell, Aldous Huxley, and Camus, leaders of a host of worshipping intelligentsia – a great galaxy of darkened stars dulling the human sky. Many of these are very fine writers indeed, but to me they seem to be setting down the history of life as a Doomsday Book, though Samuel Beckett wears his rue with a difference. He is a poet, and there is a sly humor as well as music in his writing. One has but to listen to good actors speaking it within a monologue or a play to hear the music, at times to feel the deep, gloomy compassion, and to be touched by the humor in the sad recital.[8]

Beckett, for his part, had long been an admirer of O'Casey, and this mutual admiration and respect which the two self-exiled Irishmen felt for each other speaks of a kinship of spirit and sensibility, and of an affinity which underlies their work, at least in certain clearly defined areas. In fact, long before Beckett wrote his own plays, he defined that humanly absurd element which comprises the 'essential' O'Casey:

Mr O'Casey is a master of knockabout in this very serious and honourable sense – that he discerns the principle of disintegration in even the most complacent solidities, and activates it to their explosion. This is the energy of his theatre, the triumph of the principle of knockabout in situation, in all its elements and on all its planes, from the furniture to the higher centres. If 'Juno and the Paycock,' as seems likely, is his best work so far, it is because it communicates most fully this dramatic dehiscence, mind and world come asunder in irreparable dissociation – 'chassis.'9

Beckett's interest and delight in the 'knockabout' world of O'Caseyan drama actually presages, as David Krause points out, 'the knockabout nightmare world of Gogo and Didi, Pozzo and Lucky, Hamm and Clov, Nagg and Nell, Krapp and Krapp, Winnie and Willie.'10 Moreover, Beckett's definition of O'Casey's 'chassis' as a state in which 'mind and world come asunder in irreparable dissociation' points to the fact that O'Casey's 'state o' chassis' *is*, in fact, the 'disintegrated' mode of the Absurd, with all of its tragi-comic display of metaphysical anguish. O'Casey's plays, with their knockabout, and with their basic structural metaphor of 'chassis,' suggest a relationship between the two theatres which is finally beginning to be recognized.

Thus at the end of *Juno* when the furniture removal men have literally taken the room apart before our very eyes and the drunken Boyle and Joxer struggle to keep from falling on the almost empty stage, the concrete image that results is a classic one which will appear again and again in the Theatre of the Absurd. Truly, 'The blinds is down'; there is no sunlight; man is surrounded by emptiness; he is alone, except for his 'parasite' or slave, who is, perhaps, his alter ego. Communication, too, is difficult, if not impossible, for words have become disjointed, their point of contact with reality uncertain:

> The counthry'll have to steady itself ... it's goin' ... to hell ... Where'r all ... the chairs ... gone to ... steady itself, Joxer ... Chairs'll ... have to ... steady themselves ... No matther ... what any one may ... say ... Irelan' sober ... is Irelan' ... free. (p 88)

Moreover, the ideals of Irish patriotism embodied in the fantasies of Boyle and Joxer are as insubstantial as the conjectures about Godot that preoccupy Gogo and Didi. Both worlds are absurd, but, of the two, Beckett's is the harsher, since it exists almost without reference to a saner world of basic human values, that world which Juno and Mary have, presumably, just set out to regain.

Yet the laughter which arises is, in both cases, a reaffirming laughter, for it springs from our own awareness of the discrepancy between the amount of anguish evoked and the amount which might reasonably be justified by the 'state o' chassis' that prevails. We laugh at Boyle and Joxer because, while they would enlarge the scope of their sufferings, flinging them against the grander background of Ireland's greater anguish, they are actually not even aware of the true dimensions of the 'chassis' that has invaded their lives. Boyle does not know his son is dead, nor does he — *Boyle's* realize that Juno and Mary have left him. On the contrary, all that Boyle *ignorance* and his 'butty' Joxer understand is that the money, with the comforts it provided, is gone, and so the last 'tanner' flung into the centre of the stage becomes the actual focus of their grief. Thus their anguish is ironically disproportionate to its cause: greater than its known cause – the loss of the legacy – less than what should be its real cause – the death of a son, the breaking up of a family, the Civil War in Ireland.

With Gogo and Didi, too, we have a sense of disproportion, both grotesque and humorous, a sense that their grief is somehow less than the situation warrants – or perhaps it is greater – we cannot tell which. Godot – Man – God: a mysterious trinity, to say the least. And waiting for Godot, or, like Pozzo and Lucky, not waiting, is equally futile. All that is certain is that man's life is defined by two polarities, annihilation and salvation:

> VLADIMIR We'll hang ourselves to-morrow. (*Pause.*) Unless Godot comes.
> ESTRAGON And if he comes?
> VLADIMIR We'll be saved.[11]

Yet not even this much is certain, for the words of these two sad clowns are continually contradicted by their actions, proof enough that mind and world have come irreparably asunder. And this is the way the play ends:

> VLADIMIR Well? Shall we go?
> ESTRAGON Yes, let's go.
> *They do not move.* (p 60)

As in the Theatre of the Absurd, the world Boyle and Joxer struggle comically to comprehend can be summed up, finally, only by an admission of its total incomprehensibility. 'Th' whole worl',' Boyle tells Joxer conclusively, is 'in a terr ... ible state o' ... chassis!' (p 89). It is a frightening admission, but there is an undertone of self-importance, even of triumph, in Boyle's voice, for he is one of those capable (despite the odd pratfall) of *Boyle* standing up to such an irrational and cruel universe.

In *Juno and the Paycock*, as in his other plays, O'Casey revals that he understood instinctively the Artaudian concept of a 'theatre of cruelty,' though in 'The Bald Primaqueera,' he chose instead to lampoon, in the most outrageous way he knew how, those expressions of it which he felt, perhaps rightly, invited man to despair. A similar conclusion has been reached by Robert P. Murphy, who is the first to recognize the many affinities both of dramatic motifs and dramaturgical devices between O'Casey's theatre and the theatre of Artaud. Yet Murphy does not care to speculate on why O'Casey 'seems unwilling or unable to admit that the theatre of cruelty is more than violence or the threat of violence.'[12]

In *The Theater and Its Double*, Artaud specifically comments on this oversimplified notion of cruelty (such as O'Casey deliberately fastened on), when he writes:

It is not the cruelty we can exercise upon each other by hacking at each other's bodies, carving up our personal anatomies, or, like Assyrian emperors, sending parcels of human ears, noses, or neatly detached nostrils through the mail, but the much more terrible and necessary cruelty which things can exercise against us. We are not free. And the sky can still fall on our heads. And the theater has been created to teach us that first of all.[13]

Clearly, there are many moments in the theatre of O'Casey where such a world is glimpsed. It is even possible to catalogue (as Murphy does) the surprisingly large number of gratuitous deaths that do occur in O'Casey's plays: Minnie's, in *Shadow of a Gunman*, the death of Bessie Burgess in *The Plough and the Stars*, the shooting of Ayamonn in *Red Roses for Me*, the death of Jack the lorry driver, struck down in anger by Father Domineer in *Cock-a-Doodle Dandy*, the impending death of the paralysed Julia in the same play, and the murder of Foorawn in *The Bishop's Bonfire*.

But what we should also be aware of is that as many of these deaths as possible occur offstage. In fact, O'Casey rewrote the scene in *Juno* where Johnny is taken by the IRA so that we are not even asked to visualize the actual physical violence. Instead, the news of Johnny's death is brought by two impatient policemen and conveyed sympathetically by Mrs Madigan to Juno, whose words of grief echo those of Mrs Tancred when her own son was killed because Johnny had betrayed him. Such multiple ironies are more effective than any number of casual onstage shootings and underline the senseless cruelty of a world engaged in Civil War, a world which makes its comic ascendancy in the final scene of 'chassis.' In an O'Casey play, then, when the sky does fall – as it threatened to fall on Chicken Little – the cruelty and comedy mingle as they do in the child's magical world of the nursery fable or in the celluloid world of the cartoon.

However, while both Artaud and O'Casey insist on magic in the theatre in order to express the mysterious, unknown quality of life, the effect of O'Casey's magic is quite different. To Artaud, magic is 'brimstone,' and therefore it follows that his theatre 'emphasizes the scathes, disappointments, and suffering of life.'[4] Whereas, to O'Casey: 'A play poetical to be worthy of the theatre must be able to withstand the terror of Ta Ra Ra Boom Dee Ay, as a blue sky, or an apple tree in bloom, withstand any ugliness around or beneath them.'[5] In other words, O'Casey rarely offers us straight brimstone to drink, but more often a deceptively innocent-looking mixture of brimstone and treacle – a traditional nursery medicine.

Actually, it is seldom recognized nowadays that, even in O'Casey's later plays, this kind of magic, like the drum roll of Father Ned or the trumpeting of St Trinculo in *The Bishop's Bonfire*, heralds potential danger and the risk of disaster as well as laughter, excitement, and mystery. Though at least one critic has even managed to overstate the sense of despair in *Juno*, the more usual tendency now is to overlook the very real danger that lurks in O'Casey's tragi-comic 'state o' chassis' and in his often seemingly innocent Ta Ra Ra Boom Dee Ay of life. Ironically, then, it is really only in retrospect and in the context of the Theatre of the Absurd and the Theatre of Cruelty, that Joseph Wood Krutch's comment about the final scene in *Juno* takes on its true significance: 'Like the play as a whole, this concluding scene is funny at the same time that it is bitter, hopeless, and terrible. It would, in fact, be difficult to find anywhere else in dramatic literature so extraordinary a combination of farce with loathing and a bleak despair.'[6]

And yet it is just this extraordinary combination of farce and tragic despair that threatens in *The Silver Tassie* to blot out, for once, the blue sky and the blossoms of apple tree or daffodil. Nowhere else in O'Casey is the mixture of laughter and tears so painful. Nowhere else is the juxtaposition and mingling, not only of comedy and tragedy, but also of farce and tragedy treated so masterfully and so intensely. Think, for example, of Act III, where Harry's agonized and terrified awareness of 'a soft, velvety sense of distance between my fingers and the things I touch' (p 65) expresses so completely the 'irreparable dissociation' of mind and body, of a world falling asunder into chaos. Here, certainly, is mystery and terror, and also a kind of magic, for there is magic in O'Casey's language as he surrounds Harry with scenes of comic anarchy and refuses to let him – or us – escape from the Ta Ra Ra Boom Dee Ay of life.

As Harry agonizes over his condition, life rollicks mindlessly on: 'Kiss in a corner; ta-ra-ra-ra, kiss in a corner!' (p 70). Surgeon Maxwell flirts outrageously with Susie, while deciding, at the same time, that Sylvester must be operated on in the morning, information which sends the reluctant patient into an unwarranted paroxysm of terror. Sylvester's outraged and agonized response, as he calculates the odds for survival in this kind of universe, is wildly funny. But since in this scene he functions as a kind of comic surrogate for Harry, who is also to be operated on in the morning, there are darker and more painful undertones:

> SYLVESTER We have our hands full, Simon, to keep alive. Think of sinkin' your body to the level of a hand that, ta-ra-ra-ra, would plunge a knife into your middle, haphazard, hurryin' up to run away after a thrill from a kiss in a corner. Did you see me dizzied an' wastin' me time pumpin' ninety-nines out of me, unrecognized, quiverin' with cold an' equivocation!
> SIMON Everybody says he's a very clever fellow with the knife.
> SYLVESTER He'd gouge out your eye, saw off your arm, lift a load of vitals out of your middle, rub his hands, keep down a terrible desire to cheer lookin' at the ruin, an' say, 'Twenty-six, when you're a little better, you'll feel a new man!' (pp 70–1)

It is with a start that we realize that the kind of comic mutilations described here and portrayed, on the tragic level, by the blind Teddy and the paralysed Harry are quite similar to those which abound in the Theatre of the Absurd and Theatre of Cruelty. The absurdists, in fact, have populated their plays with blind, deaf, dumb, and crippled creatures, perhaps the most grotesque of which is the protagonist of Adamov's *La grande et la petite manœuvre*, who loses one limb after another each time he shows some kind of weakness, until he ends up as a basket case in a wheelchair and is then pushed under a truck. Clearly, what these very sad clowns are trying to tell us is that the human condition is one of impotence in the face of a universe that is implacably cruel and mysterious.

It is the same theme heard in Gloucester's anguished cry,

> As flies to wanton boys, are we to the gods.
> They kill us for their sport.

Yet, in the world of the absurdists, the gods are not simply unjust and inscrutable: they no longer even exist, and those who, like Mullcanny in

Red Roses for Me, have made the 'grand discovery' that 'God is dead' (p 151) can now draw two totally opposite conclusions.

In the face of such a meaningless universe, where the sky can fall at any moment and where there is so much suffering, one conclusion we can obviously come to is that life has no meaning. Thus, in the world depicted by the absurdists, man's intelligent and rational speech becomes, finally, an unintelligible cry. Harold Pinter's *The Birthday Party*, for example, shows Stanley gagging on such a world when Goldberg and McCann offer it to him for his birthday:

> GOLDBERG Well, Stanny boy, what do you say, eh?
> *They watch. He concentrates. His head lowers, his chin draws into his chest, he crouches.*
> STANLEY Ug-gughh ... uh-gughh ...
> MCCANN What's your opinion, sir?
> STANLEY Caaahhh ... caaahhh ... [17]

The closest we come to this kind of huddled and despairing cry in the theatre of O'Casey is in Harry's bitter denial, 'Napoo!' (pp 91, 101; 'Vanished! lost! done! finished!'), a denial of home and friend and the girl he loves – all now equally meaningless. If the word was not already becoming obsolete when O'Casey used it, he must nevertheless have chosen it for the quality of its sound. For its power, in the context of the Theatre of the Absurd, also derives, perhaps coincidentally, from its very strangeness, its very unintelligibility. By contrast, the anguished crying of Ayamonn's name, which occurs several times throughout the final act of *Red Roses for Me* (pp 222, 224), functions on both a realistic and expressionist level to present a world which, in its Easter-time context, is simultaneously absurd and divine.

Here, then, is the other conclusion that we can come to in a meaningless universe: man must create his own meaning, must continually make his own affirmations. This task is not an easy one, and it comes as no surprise to discover that the anguish of the absurdists is often reflected in their lives, as well as in their plays. Certainly this is true of Ionesco, Adamov, and Genêt, though the example of Artaud, himself, with his visions and his history of mental breakdown, is the most extreme. Significantly, however, it is in O'Casey's plays, rather than in the plays of the absurdists, that we can detect something of Artaud's messianic vision.

Somewhat paradoxically, Artaud believed, as did O'Casey, that the true theatrical experience was a religious one, that the experience of the theatre was a communion involving all its participants, and that to base the drama in myth and ritual was to root it in life itself. Such plays as *The Silver Tassie* and *Red Roses for Me* are particularly good illustrations of what Artaud meant when he wrote: 'To break through language in order to touch life is to create or recreate the theater':

Furthermore, when we speak the word 'life,' it must be understood we are not referring to life as we know it from its surface of fact, but to that fragile, fluctuating center which forms never reach. And if there is still one hellish, truly accursed thing in our time, it is our artistic dallying with forms, instead of being like victims burnt at the stake, signaling through the flames.[18]

The ultimately unbearable intensity of Artaud's artistic vision is summed up by the metaphor of fire. Whereas, in O'Casey, it is not so much the metaphor of fire, as of light – from the 'red glare' illuminating the darkness in Act II of *The Silver Tassie* to the 'little flower of light' that the lamplighter carries in *Red Roses for Me* – which best expresses the range and intensity of O'Casey's vision.

And it is somewhere between the burning genius of Artaud and the brilliant illumination of O'Casey's genius that we glimpse the countenance of Beckett as Martin Esslin describes him, 'the most balanced and serene of men.'[19] Of all the absurdists, it is Beckett who allows us to catch almost infinitesimal glimmers of hope in the midst of darkest despair: the 'four or five leaves' that have suddenly appeared on the tree in the second act of *Godot*, for instance, or the fact that, after innumerable pratfalls, Gogo and Didi are standing miraculously upright at the final curtain – and Gogo has even managed to pull up his trousers!

To evoke laughter in the face of despair and to make poetry out of the cruelty of the human condition is a considerable achievement. For O'Casey, however, it was clearly not enough. And if the escatic joy which transforms the hearts of the Dublin men and women in the visionary third act of *Red Roses for Me* occurs only once, there are still many times in the theatre of O'Casey where the possibility of such a transfigured world is glimpsed. For it is just where his vision is darkest and the irony most intense that O'Casey's characters usually choose to affirm life in whatever way they can.

Even in *The Silver Tassie*, the darkest of all O'Casey's plays, Harry, the grotesque 'half-baked Lazarus' (p 199), is finally able to put his wits together long enough to make sense out of nonsense: 'The Lord hath given and man hath taken away!' Of course, in the context of blind man and wheelchair victim, Harry's previous resolve, 'What's in front we'll face like men!' (p 102) – as its deliberately trite and commonplace phrasing confirms – seems as ironic and futile as any of the attempts at affirmation made by Gogo and Didi. In fact, it is really only in the final movement of Harry and Teddy onstage, more than in their speech, that we can discern the more positive direction that the O'Casey play takes. For, in the last two acts of *The Tassie*, the garden on the edge of the 'wilderness' exists, for the most part, outside the consciousness of the characters in the play. Or, at any rate, the garden exists on the very periphery of consciousness (like the calm sea in *Endgame*), related only tangentially to the world of the absurd that dominates the stage. Thus, as blind man and cripple move into the garden prior to going offstage altogether, this purposeful movement, in contrast to the immobility of Gogo and Didi, or Hamm and Clov, at their play's end, must be seen as some kind of rather less ambiguous affirmation.

In *Endgame*, moreover, the actions of Hamm and Clov finally negate the positive direction in which the play, even if only by means of its often lyrical dialogue, is attempting to move. Nagg's generosity to Nell, for example, is continually thwarted by Hamm's orders, which Clov faithfully carries out: stuffed in ash-cans, Nagg and Nell cannot move close enough together to kiss, or to scratch each other's backs. For Hamm, in his misery, is destructive and has been responsible for the deaths of the other survivors. In fact his cruelty to others is appalling. But since it springs directly from the terrible way in which a cruel and senseless universe has treated him, it is, like Harry Heegan's cruelty, easily understandable.

Yet, while Hamm controls the others, he is impotent: blind and paralyzed, wheeled about in an armchair with castors, he calls petulantly for his pain-killer and his catheter. For he is another of the maimed creatures of the Absurd whose multiple disabilities embody a gaping spiritual defect. Nor is there any cure for what is simply part of the human condition. As Hamm reminds Clov: 'use your head, can't you, use your head, you're on earth, there's no cure for that!'[20]

With Hamm, despair continually extinguishes hope, even as it continually points to the existence of that cruel and absurd universe from which man so longs to escape. The image of Hamm in his wheelchair, then, is one of the most basic images of the Absurd: man reduced to 'ham,'[21] to the purely animal and physical, by means of a despair which overwhelms and finally annihilates him. The image is becoming a familiar one in our time, as it sums up all the metaphysical anguish of twentieth-century man in a mechanized world. Impotent, blind, crippled, without faith or hope, unable any longer to walk upright, he lashes out angrily at whatever crosses his path.

And behind the figure of Hamm, if we look closely, is the figure of another wheelchair victim – Harry Heegan – wheeling himself crazily about the stage, pursuing, running down and grappling with whatever he thinks to be the cause of his anguish, and, finally, calling out, both to man and God, for the misery to cease. And though the torment can never cease for Harry Heegan, it does lessen, partly because he has plumbed the limits of despair and can go no further, but also because, by an act of faith or will, he chooses to move into the garden – beyond the Absurd.

It is these limits which both the Theatre of O'Casey and the Theatre of the Absurd continually re-examine and redefine. But, while 'The blinds is down' (p 88) for Captain Boyle and his 'butty' Joxer, the darkness is not nearly so intense as that which ends Hamm's apocalyptic day: 'You cried for night; it falls: now cry in darkness' (p 83). Hamm's words are a poignant and lyrical description of one aspect of the human condition, but the advice would never be followed by an O'Casey character simply because – with such rare exceptions as Nora Clitheroe and Harry Heegan – an O'Casey character never gives in, for long, to despair.

THE DISINTEGRATED MODE OF THE ABSURD

O'Casey's relationship to the Theatre of the Absurd, made apparent first of all by his use of such key structural images as the 'state o' chassis' and man in a wheelchair, is also clearly evident in the particular way he uses language. The 'irreparable dissociation' of mind and world that puzzles and amazes Boyle and terrifies Harry finds concrete expression, not only in disintegrating stage sets, in the splitting apart of families, in violent quarrels, in blind and crippled bodies, in sudden, gratuitous deaths, but also, above all, in the violent rending apart of language itself, a convulsion that can result, however, in a new world of meaning rising out of the old. Accordingly, by the end of *Red Roses for Me*, even Brennan's ridiculous cliché, 'Money's the root of all evil' (p 211), is forced to impart its own unexpected truth. And what is revealed is that to choose Brennan's viewing of life – or, worse still, the Inspector's – is to choose to live in a world of cliché and absurdity. Such an ironic use of the cliché is a characteristic device of O'Casey's from the early plays onward. In *Juno and the Paycock*, for example, the hackneyed slogan 'a principle's a principle' (p 8) echoes throughout the play, but before it is over the actions of the various characters have exposed, and rejected, the hollowness of a world which tries to function according to completely arbitrary and inhuman principles.

Similarly, in *The Bald Prima Donna*, Ionesco uses cliché to record the pettiness, meanness, viciousness – and, finally, the absurdity – of the world his characters inhabit. But, again, the difference between the two theatres is one of degree. For Ionesco, unlike O'Casey, often makes his characters speak nothing but cliché, so that, in effect, a process of *reductio ad absurdum* is constantly at work. Is it any wonder, then, that Ionesco's plays evoked the charge that language is in the process of being broken down and stripped of meaning altogether?[22] Yet Ionesco denied that he felt language had become meaningless: 'The very fact of writing and presenting plays is surely incompatible with such a view. I simply hold that it is difficult to make oneself understood, not absolutely impossible.'[23]

Ionesco's reply makes clear that the difficulty of communicating new ideas in a language which has become riddled with clichés, truisms, and the slogans of outworn ideologies is, of course, basically the same for any writer. But what links O'Casey ahead to Ionesco and the Absurdists, rather than back to Toller and the Expressionists, is the fact that O'Casey is not afraid to satirize verbal formulas – to disintegrate language along with the stage sets – since he knows that, in the explosion which follows, a lot of false beliefs and prejudices will be swept away. Thus, while the basic device which O'Casey uses to force language to communicate again is the old, traditional one of dramatic irony, he often pushes it to an extreme which creates a new context: one which can replace walls with the limitless perspective of the universe.

In this universe stumble characters who reveal, by the emptiness of their nonsensical conversations, their mental and spiritual disabilities. Such characters, with their use of obscure and unpronounceable names or Latin tags – 'Terra Del Fooaygeeans,' 'os coccyges' – even manage to *sound* like fugitives on their way from the expressionist theatre of O'Casey to the Theatre of the Absurd. However, while these various kinds of 'talkathons' – so characteristic of both theatres – usually sound quite funny and seem harmless enough, they can at times be harmful, and, at worst, downright dangerous. Not only do they signify the 'blindness' and 'impotence' of certain characters, but they can also signify a willingness to blind and castrate others, if not to destroy them completely. For example, the Professor in Ionesco's *The Lesson* and McCann and Goldberg in Pinter's *The Birthday Party* destroy their victims, first of all, by talk. And the final disastrous result of all this empty and dangerous talk is the realization onstage of a dark and crippled world, a world which can be summed up in the images of blind man and wheelchair victim.

Disintegrated language, then, itself becomes one of the most basic images of a world which continually threatens us with its unintelligibility. And cliché, platitude, political slogans, mispronounced words, or words from dead or foreign languages are but a few of the many modes of its disintegration which O'Casey shares with the absurdists. Yet, rather than merely acknowledging and confronting such an unintelligible universe, O'Casey actively persists in his attempts to find new ways of establishing meaning. In Act III of *The Tassie*, to take a more complex example, the extremely intricate effect of the repetition of the name 'Sister Peter Alcantara' five times in seven lines of dialogue comes from the interaction of words and rhythm:

> MRS HEEGAN Sister Peter Alcantara said we might come up, Nurse.
> MRS FORAN (*loftily*) Sister Peter Alcantara's authority ought to be good enough, I think.
> MRS HEEGAN Sister Peter Alcantara said a visit might buck him up a bit.
> MRS FORAN Sister Peter Alcantara knows the responsibility she'd incur by keeping a wife from her husband and a mother from her son.
> SUSIE Sister Peter Alcantara hasn't got to nurse him. (p 71)

This apparently senseless and farcical repetition of a name is the kind of repetition that fequently occurs in the dialogue of Absurd plays. It is another one of the many devices which signal that the characters are having difficulty in communicating. And it occurs as a prelude to the 'Disgraceful ... commotion' (p 75) – the 'state o' chassis' – into which the visiting scene collapses. Thus, despite the assurances, the repeated affirmation in the appeal to the authority of a representative of the Church, the dissonant note struck by Susie's reply has been carried all along in the rhythmical drumbeat of the name in which the militant power of the Church itself is felt. In the rhythms of the name – Sís-těr Pé-těr Ál-căn-tá-ră – there is more of O'Casey's Ta Ra Ra Boom Dee Ay of life with its attendant dangers. Here, the rhythms should remind us that it is the powerful authority of the Church militant that has countenanced the war in which Harry has been crippled and Teddy blinded. For the characters onstage, however, the language communicates on only the most elementary level. And the constant repetitions, like those in a child's primer (or the English language primer out of which Ionesco constructed *The Bald Prima Donna*), calls attention to this fact.

Yet it is out of our awareness of the disintegration of their language and the explosion of laughter that results from their absurdity that O'Casey manages to make sense. In other words, by using one of the disintegrated fragments of language, in this case, the rhythms and tonal qualities of the words themselves, O'Casey forces language to communicate again. And what we should hear in the persistent repetition of the name, 'Sister Peter Alcantara' – and what the director should perhaps let us hear in the wings – is the insistent drumbeat of war.

Finally, the complex use O'Casey makes of dialect illustrates even more clearly the artifice that is involved in creating 'humanly absurd' characters whose speech is supposedly a faithful transcript of life. Even in the early plays, as J.A. Snowden comments, O'Casey 'shows a preoccupation with language and an obvious belief in its power to transform reality.'[24] By the time he is writing *Red Roses*, O'Casey is using dialect (or the absence of dialect) for symbolic purposes, to convey a mood or attitude or a metaphysical dimension of character. For example, during the religious dissension in Act II, Brennan, who usually speaks like a Dubliner, lapses into a 'semi-Ulster' dialect. Similarly, Foster and Dowzard speak in a strong Ulster dialect – so characteristic of the extreme Orange faction – though there is no indication in the text that they come from anywhere else but Dublin. What O'Casey is doing, then, is using the dialect to indicate an attitude of extreme fanaticism where religious matters are concerned, an attitude which is not confined to Ulster, but which can be found anywhere. Since the dialect is broken apart, as it were, from its normal referent and used satirically and symbolically, it provides still another instance of language being used in the disintegrated mode of the Absurd.

The apparent contradiction which underlies the fact that such a disintegration of language has resulted in some of the most vital of contemporary theatre, together with dialogue that is fresh and new and really very exciting, is a contradiction which can be resolved by recognizing that disintegrating language, like laughter itself, is a liberating process. O'Casey seems to have realized this instinctively and was never averse to playing exuberantly with language for fear it might drop and break. On the contrary, especially in his persona of the raucous Green Crow, he became quite vocal in his demands for a liberated theatre, one in which there is the freedom to mix styles and modes, prose and verse, dialects and rhetorical devices with what may look at first like a kind of gay abandon. What we need to be aware of, however, in evaluating O'Casey's apparent 'excesses' of language, is that there may be a legitimate dramatic purpose behind his use of sentimental or melodramatic cliché, or behind his use of what has been called a 'pseudo-poetic' rhetoric. And that purpose, as well as his means of realizing it onstage, can often be made clear in the light of the Absurd.

POETRY IN SPACE

While some of O'Casey's language (like some of his stage sets) shows a remarkable inclination to fly apart, his stagecraft, by contrast, shows a remarkable cohesiveness. It is, in fact, his skilful use of all the elements of theatre, particularly in his two most visionary plays, that often allows him to build a series of concrete symbolic images, all closely integrated, which, if properly realized onstage, will unify what otherwise can wrongly appear as a loosely knit and disparate structure.

Moreover, the way in which O'Casey uses the concrete 'physical' aspects of his theatre – dance, mime and mask, music, lighting, and scenery – bears a striking resemblance to the way in which the exponents of the Theatre of Cruelty have made use of Artaud's concept of *mise en scène*.[25] This relationship can be discerned, for instance, in the various transformation scenes and in the dances of life – or death – found throughout the O'Casey canon, each of which can be described as an 'Artaudian replacement of words by another dramatic language.'[26] Though in the final analysis, O'Casey's language is never really devaluated, in this kind of 'speech before words' the appeal is clearly to the senses and cannot be fully articulated by the dialogue alone.

Thus, in his own attempts to break the bonds of the realistic stage, O'Casey was actually translating into practical stagecraft, even earlier than 1928, a great many of the less extreme demands that Artaud was to formulate, with messianic zeal, a decade later. Ironically, though O'Casey was to make his demands clearly enough and in a way which linked his theatre to the traditions of the past – to the 'big life and ... gorgeous time' that the theatre had 'when the Trade Guilds went about in their wagons doing the Mystery and the Morality Plays,'[27] and to the exuberance and freedom of the Elizabethan stage – the true nature of his experimental drama was constantly obscured by the criticism (often sectarian and non-literary) which assailed it.

But if we use Ionesco's articulate and far-reaching claims for the contemporary avant-garde theatre as a kind of lens to view, in retrospect, the plays of Sean O'Casey, what we confirm is how surprisingly alike, in their use of certain elements of stagecraft, the two theatres are:

Everything is permitted in the theatre: to bring characters to life, but also to materialize states of anxiety, inner presences. It is thus not only permitted, but advisable, to make the properties join in the action, to make objects live, to animate the décor, to make symbols concrete. Just as words are continued by gesture, action, mime, which, at the moment when words become inadequate, take their place, the material elements of the stage can in turn further intensify these.[28]

This kind of theatre, where *mise en scène* is itself the essence of the drama, has been described as 'concretized poetic images in associative sequence,' a concept which is an elaboration of Artaud's own term, 'poetry in space.'[29] What better way could one describe the total effect of, say, Act II of *The Silver Tassie* or Act III of *Red Roses*? Certainly what unifies these two acts, when plot and character apparently become fluid and disunified (perhaps we should say 'disintegrated'), is the highly formal structure that unifies poetry.

Thinking of Absurd plays as 'poems,' Esslin calls attention to the symmetry of Acts I and II of *Waiting for Godot* and 'the rigid ritual structure of *The Blacks*.'[30] Clearly, the formal and dramatic structure of *The Tassie* also depends upon the symmetry of the ritual: the symmetrical 'elevations' both of 'chalice' and 'host,' the 'host' being Harry in Act I, the Croucher in Act II. While in *Red Roses*, as we have seen, the underlying formal principle, made evident by its Easter setting, is that of the miracle or passion play.

The inclusion, once again, in the theatre of such formal elements as myth and ritual has naturally tended to acquire a certain aura of respectability: whereas the inclusion of such apparently disparate elements as those drawn from the circus, the ballet, the mime show, or the music hall – at least until the advent of the absurdists – has not. And yet the effect of adding these magical elements to a basically realistic theatre, as O'Casey was apparently aware, is to give more scope to the expression of the absurd side of man's nature. The portrayal which results is often a grotesque, yet by taking into full account the basest aspect of our humanity, and by liberating us from it by laughter, such a portrayal also has the capacity for showing forth the sublime. Characters, scenes, and images which are grotesque are, in fact, one of O'Casey's means of realizing onstage the most complete dimensions of man's life and of the world he inhabits.

For O'Casey's artistic vision saw how the grotesque images of the Expressionists could be used in a new way: one in which elements of farce, as an expression and admission of the absurd side of our nature, can heighten, as well as shatter, our sense of the tragic, the noble or the divine. Thus, in *Red Roses*, a play whose affinities with the Absurd derive directly from O'Casey's own 'homemade' expressionism, he fully acknowledges, in Ayamonn's 'hunchbacked' form, our bondage in an unintelligible world in order to show us why such a world must somehow be translated.

From early plays to late, O'Casey's tragi-comic vision naturally found expression in a multiplicity of grotesque and absurd images: from Bessie's dishevelled head (framed in a tenement window), crying, 'Choke th' chicken,' to the mysteriously appearing statue in *Figuro in the Night*. Yet, of all these images, it is one from *Red Roses for Me*, 'the severed head of Dunn-Bo speaking out of the darkness' (p 198), which best sums up that quality of O'Casey's work that has remained without a proper critical context or vocabulary to explicate it. Labelled simply as 'a piece of near-expressionist symbolism,'[31] the severed head has been reduced to 'atmosphere' with something like the melodramatic effect of the grave-yard scene in Wedekind's *Spring's Awakening*, where Moritz 'comes stomping over the graves, his head under his arm.'[32] In fact this part of the transformation scene has consistently been dramatized in a way which topples the act, and, frequently, much of the play into bathos and sentimentality. As well as being bathed in 'a patch of supernatural light descending from the sky like a benediction,'[33] the head of Dunn-Bo demands to be realized onstage in a way which does not understate its relationship to the 'severed' heads of Nagg and Nell as they come popping up out of the ashcans in *Endgame*, or the head of Winnie resting atop the mound of earth in *Happy Days*.

However, it is out of this absurd world (as he modulates through the grotesque on the way to the sublime) that O'Casey, unlike Beckett, creates *onstage* a new world of meaning. Thus the severed head of Dunn-Bo, contrary to what we would expect, does not prophesy, except by speaking in the apparently meaningless cliché of political rhetoric – 'A step ahead for us today: another one for you tomorrow' (p 198) – and so calls into doubt its own role as a symbol of the godhead. Here is Ayamonn apparently 'talking' himself to his death, foolishly giving his life, as the severed head so mockingly implies, for the ideals he believes in. Yet, the next moment, moving beyond parody, the head appears magical, prophetic, and divine as Ayamonn's empty rhetoric is replaced by 'poetry in space,' poetry made concrete by the miraculous transformation of the world about him. For the ecstatic dance of life in which Ayamonn and Finnoola now join is the celebration of a world which is no longer absurd.

But it is when we are without such a vision that life can quickly become a macabre dance of death: Dowzard dancing wildly about as he shouts, 'Th' dhrum, th' dhrum, th' Protestant dhrum!' (p 220), or Foster, 'a dancing dervish,'[34] trampling on Ayamann's cross of daffodils; or Harry in his wheelchair crying, 'Trumpets and drum begin! ... Dance and dance and dance', as he 'Whirls round ... to the beat of the tune' (p 93). In each case the dancing is a maimed and crippled rite, a St Vitus dance of pained, spasmodic movements, the grotesque convulsions of those who are possessed, not by a sense of love and fellowship, but by an agonizing hatred of their fellow man.

Not so surprisingly, then, while both visionary plays struggle to transcend despair, it is in the more anguished *Tassie*, when Harry, despite his 'agony,' is able to move into the garden, that the absurd world remains behind to dominate the stage. Whereas, it is in *Red Roses* (*The Tassie*'s 'mirror twin'), when Foster and Dowzard flee in terror out of the garden taking with them their absurd world of buffoonery and knockabout, that Ayamonn's vision, caught in the harmony of song, presents, as the curtain falls, a final image of *discordia concors*.

TO THE SOUND OF TRUMPET AND DRUM:
THE THEATRE OF O'CASEY

What distinguishes O'Casey's vision from that of either the Expressionists or the Absurdists is this unerring ability to harmonize discords, to integrate successfully both thematically and in terms of stagecraft, all the wildly disintegrating elements of the world in which we live. Unlike Ernst Toller, who, in *Transfiguration*, could not control the effect of farce in the dance of death with the girl skeleton 'outraged' by war,[35] O'Casey was able to mingle the absurd and the tragic – in the 'graveyard' scene in Act II of *The Tassie*, for example – to heighten and make credible his overall artistic purpose. But the effect of farce mingling with tragedy was one that audiences in the late twenties were almost completely unprepared for, as the rejection of *The Tassie* and the ensuing controversy made plain.

When an Expressionist skeleton appears in a dance of death on an English stage just prior to the sixties, however, a change has taken place, both in the play and in the audience. The play is John Arden's *Serjeant Musgrave's Dance* – that one 'Primaqueera' play which O'Casey exempted from his wholesale condemnation because, undoubtedly, he recognized in it an artistic vision akin to his own. Much of the power of the Arden play comes, in fact, from his use of the grotesque: Serjeant Musgrave expresses his despair and rage and his desire for revenge in a macabre dance of death, performed, appropriately enough, to the warlike sound of trumpet and drum. The point of the scene is underlined by having the hanging, dancing skeleton unveiled as the 'flag' beneath which Serjeant Musgrave himself dances, 'his face contorted with demoniac fury.'[36] The skeleton is that of a comrade killed senselessly in a guerilla-type encounter and brought back to his home town in the box that the Serjeant and the other deserters have been carrying throughout the play. Thus the skeleton has not been brought in as a kind of portable 'atmosphere' but has been skilfully integrated into the narrative and dramatic structure. In this way, Arden's grotesque image of the dance of death now seems to bear a more direct relationship to O'Casey's 'h⁻ memade' expressionism – O'Casey's own 'poetry in space' – than it does to the Expressionist stage.

Significantly, it is in the work of such a playwright as Arden that Martin Esslin sees most clearly the direction in which contemporary drama should develop. In *Serjeant Musgrave's Dance*, Esslin discerns the bringing together of those elements of fable, folksong, and picaresque incident that are characteristic of Brecht's theatre with 'the obsessiveness, the nightmarish psychological reality of the Theatre of the Absurd – without ever leaving the plane of external realism.'[37] Moreover, it is these two wings of the avant-garde – the objective, realistic, socially committed epic theatre of Brecht and the subjective, poetic, grotesque drama of the absurdists – that Esslin credits with rescuing the theatre from the bonds of the realistic stage:

It is the achievement of the Absurdists together with the Brechtians to have brought the theatre back to the full richness of its traditional vocabulary, to have freed it from the narrow restrictionism of pretending to be reality observed through a missing fourth wall, which ... banished all the delicious world of the dreamlike, the supernatural, and its stage machinery from the theatre.[38]

The description of the theatre of the future which Esslin gives sounds so much like O'Casey's theatre that it is sometimes difficult to understand why the true nature of O'Casey's innovative craftsmanship – developing out of Expressionism and moving towards the Theatre of the Absurd –

has so long gone unrecognized. And yet a theatre which is ahead of its time can only wait patiently – or impatiently, as O'Casey did – for the times to catch up to it.

With a start we realize that all those wild and magical elements for which O'Casey's plays have long been criticized have nevertheless been accepted in the 'no-holds-barred'[39] theatre of the newer and more popular avant-garde. Their dark vision, too, has held the stage to the exclusion of O'Casey's brighter one, yet, ironically, when O'Casey's own vision was darkest – in *The Tassie–* it was rejected. And though the proportion of nightmare and obsession in the later O'Casey lessens, as does the degree of tragedy, these qualities, which dominate in the tortured characters of the absurdists, have never been lacking in O'Casey's theatre: from the tap-tapping on the wall in *Shadow of a Gunman*; through the weird prophesies of Bessie Burgess in *The Plough*, the despairing Black Mass of the Croucher, the agonizing *danse macabre* of Harry in his wheelchair, the severed head of Dunn-Bo speaking out of the darkness; and, finally, in Foster's and Dowzard's diabolical dance of death.

Part of the excitement in O'Casey's theatre depends, not only upon such grotesque scenes and characters – at times closely related to the predominantly black magic, or 'brimstone,' of the Artaudian universe – but also upon the kinds of magical transformations that a no-holds-barred theatre is free to encourage. While O'Casey lampooned Ionesco for changing people into rhinoceroses, his own fanciful creation, the cock of *Cock-a-Doodle Dandy*, is obviously a similar kind of magical stage device.[40] Then, too, the shock effect which Amos Kenan generates in *The Lion*,[41] as the baby who is building a wall of wooden blocks, brusquely changes into a general overseeing a battle and then into a building magnate, is not entirely unlike the startling effects more realistically generated by O'Casey as football hero changes to soldier, soldier to Croucher, later to the dehumanized, anonymous soldier worshipping the gun; and, finally, to wheelchair victim. In O'Casey, though many of these transformations verge on the supernatural, they have a concreteness and a reality which is too often absent from the more abstract dreamlike representations of either the Expressionist stage or the stage of the Absurd.

Throughout O'Casey's constantly changing dramatic world there is, nevertheless, an underlying sense of permanence and reality which is borne out in the context of three O'Casey plays – *The Tassie, Red Roses*, and *The Moon Shines on Kylenamoe* – written over a period of more than thirty years. In these plays one image undergoes several startling transformations to suggest, not only the changing mood and tempo, but also the vast range and harmony of O'Casey's artistic vision. Thus that agonizingly bitter-'sweet chariot' of which Harry Heegan sings is transformed, by the power of Ayamonn's vision, to a bronze 'chariot ... forging forward to th' battle-front,' until at last it becomes 'a turf creel-cart pulled by a donkey,' as a character to whom O'Casey gives his own name, Sean, 'unable to resist the humour of it ... lilts':

> Sweet chariot, comin' for to carry me home,
> Swe-et char-i-o-t, comin' for to carry me home![42]

From the tragi-comic and grotesque, through the lyrical and sublime, O'Casey comes to rest in a gently comic viewing of man. With all his ridiculous pretensions and his vices and with all his noisy quarrelsomeness, there is still something noble and divine in man which allows him to respond gratefully to life, as Lord Leslieson does to the hospitable Martha of Kylenamoe, 'Thank you, thank you, an' God save you and your good man kindly, too' (p 157). Spoken after a quarrel over nothing – in a play which, like the plays of the absurdists, gives no plot and no external motivation for its characters – these words go beyond the absurd to affirm life in a way that, for a writer who was an avowed atheist in his eightieth year, is a truly astonishing achievement.

And the fullest expression of this achievement is, clearly, the colourful host of the characters themselves, as – at the sound of trumpet and drum – they come dancing across O'Casey's Bridge of Vision to take their place amidst all the gorgeous Ta Ra Ra Boom Dee Ay of life.

APPENDIX / NOTES / BIBLIOGRAPHY / INDEX

Appendix:
Notes for Production

Since it may seem increasingly contradictory to suggest that O'Casey's stage directions should be followed exactly, and then, the next moment, to introduce innovations, it should be noted at the outset that none of the devices suggested here contradict any of the given stage directions. Rather, the devices suggest themselves in the images and texts of each scene when considered in relation to the organic form of the play as a whole. They do not introduce new images, but serve only to make explicit, and thus intensify, those which are already implicitly there.

In other words, such innovations are the conscious development of a process which began with the first production of *The Tassie* at the Apollo Theatre in 1929. It was this production which saw the elevation of the Croucher in Act II, an innovation which O'Casey carefully incorporated into the Stage Version of the text. It was this production, too, which brought Harry onstage elevated on the shoulders of his friends, a practice which was to become – as O'Casey may have foreseen – a stage tradition. Since its first performance, then, *The Silver Tassie* has been reshaping itself onstage, struggling, as it were, almost of its own accord, to reach that final perfection of form which O'Casey, for whatever reason, seemed unable at that time to achieve.

Accordingly, the further innovations suggested here are an attempt to understand, and articulate, the *genius loci* of the play, itself. Rather than radically altering the play's structure, rather than producing Act II as a separate work, or leaving it out altogether, and 'mov[ing] straight from the second to the fourth act, thus making *The Silver Tassie* a three-act play,'¹ there is, as I have already noted, a much less extreme solution which involves simply: 1/ the doubling of the roles of Harry Heegan and the Croucher (something the Apollo production had begun working towards when the actor who played Harry was also cast as the 1st Soldier); 2/ the clarification of the stage directions concerning the placement of Harry's hospital bed; and 3/ the highlighting of the major structural images of the play by whatever devices are feasible. All three innovations, of course, fall quite rightly within the domain of any director.

In *The Silver Tassie*, the gigantic image of the Croucher which dominates the stage in Act II is reflected throughout the play in multiple images of crouched and huddled figures. Thus, in retrospect, we realize that even in Act I where Harry Heegan enters, carried triumphantly on the shoulders of his friends, there should be just a hint of what is to come. The heights to which Harry has risen are too great: there is already a premonition that he will fall. The friends who carry him may stumble because he is heavy and they are noticeably tired; likely the doorway is too low, and he must crouch down in order to enter the room; and, as he proudly indicates where Jessie is to place the silver tassie, he leans forward slightly so that, again, we catch a fleeting glimpse of an elevated crouching figure.

On the comic level we realize, also in retrospect, that the 'vaudeville' scene of 'Sylvester and Mrs Foran under the Bed'[2] involves stooped and crouching figures, including, of course, Teddy Foran's.

In the second act the soldiers enter 'in a close mass,' huddled together so that, like the Croucher, they, too, project a larger than life-size image of weariness and despair.[3] As the fire in the brazier flickers and the Black Mass continues, the shadow of the Croucher – like the shadow of the Angel of Death – lengthens eerily against the sky or against a section of the ruined monastery wall.

Farce mingles with despair when the Visitor enters: 'his head is bent between his shoulders, and his shoulders are crouched a little' (p 40). The Visitor crouches for a moment as he goes to strike a match against the dangling arm of the partially fallen Christ (p 46). As each soldier cries out in protest, he rises to an upright position and then returns to a more 'reclining' position around the fire.

At the end of the act the corporal crouches slightly, though he remains standing, as he leads the obeisance to the gun. The soldiers who load and fire the gun are slightly, yet visibly, crouched. As the curtain falls, all – with the exception of Barney – wear gas masks: all are bestial, inhuman figures. The image of crouching literally fills the stage.

Only Barney retains a semblance of humanity in this insane and bestial landscape. The effect will be more grotesque, the horror more intense, if the soldiers who move to fire the gun first push the gun wheel so that it revolves partly across the stage. And Barney revolves with it, absurdly, frighteningly caught on the wheel – the rack. Then, while the soldiers put on their gas masks and join in the obeisance to the gun – and while the Croucher rises and descends from the ramp to join them – Barney grins crazily, chants madly in the upside-down world into which he has suddenly been thrust.

The effect will be grotesque yet, at the same time, the audience, inexplicably, should want to laugh. If not, the image will be unbearable. Their laughter is cut short, however, by the sudden appearance of Harry, whose agonized face disappears the next moment behind the dehumanizing gas mask. If this innovation is used, the turning of the gun wheel should be in the direction of the Croucher; the timing should be exact so that the device will serve to rivet our attention on Harry in that split second when he appears before us.

Thus Act II prepares for the frenzied and despairing figure which dominates the second half of the play: the image of the crippled Harry, wheeling himself crazily about the stage. In fact, the power generated in Act II by the gigantic image of despair which the Croucher embodies is contained and intensified now by the distraught and menacing figure of Harry crouched in the wheelchair.

The wheelchair is huge, the largest one available, with immense wheels, so the effect, at times, can be overwhelming: the threat from the Juggernaut is real and terrible. A brass crucifix may be caught in one wheel or, at its centre, the spokes may be structured to form a cross. Such a device would help to recall, from Act II, the 'crucified' figure of Barney undergoing field punishment: one of the victims of war flung beneath the wheels of the Juggernaut.

These devices, if used, should function on a subliminal level, on the level of a 'heightened' reality. The same is true of whatever devices are used in the hospital scene.

In Act III the hospital bed will better suit the purpose of the scene if it is a very high one so that Harry, again, is elevated. The crosspieces are recognizable crosses. The bed should not only be at stage right but also as close to the downstage area as can be arranged. This innovation suggests itself partly because, however we read O'Casey's own stage directions, Harry's hospital bed ends up on top of Simon's and Sylvester's. But when Harry's bed is at stage right, perhaps at right angles to the wall with the fireplace (rather than the back wall), the symmetry between Act II and the Juggernaut scene will be heightened to the point where the relationship between the Croucher and Harry begins to impinge upon the consciousness of the audience. Though the parallels must not be crudely obvious, a genuinely painful shock of recognition – to confirm what we thought we glimpsed at the end of Act II – should be achieved. This second 'recognition' scene is the climax of the play and satisfies both dramatically and aesthetically our need for understanding the kind of diabolical transformation that Harry has undergone, and for recognizing in Harry the tortured figure that dominated the stage in Act II.

The three elevations, then, can be seen to be an essential part of the complex realistic and symbolic structures that O'Casey presents onstage. As such, their effective realization in the theatre depends upon an understanding of O'Casey's stagecraft in which each room, each door, each window, each bed can have a symbolic, as well as a realistic, function. (Remember, O'Casey says: 'A house on a stage can never be a house, and that which represents it must always be a symbol. A room in a realistic play must always be a symbol for a room.'[4])

For this reason the greatest care must be taken to recreate the stage sets which O'Casey designs. There have been productions of *The Tassie*, for example, in which the outside door in Act I has been placed at stage left, whereas it should be at stage right exactly as O'Casey describes: 'another door which gives access to the rest of the house and the street, [is] on the right' (p 5); and, because this direction is so important, the positioning of the door is repeated: Susie 'is standing motionless, listening intently, looking towards the door on right' (p 6).[5] When the door is in the correct place, then Harry's symbolic entrance will also be in the correct place: downstage right, the same area in which the Croucher is elevated in Act II, approximately the same area in which the Juggernaut scene takes place in Act III.

Whatever stage business is given Harry, he should not be taken down from his elevated position too soon. The image needs time to implant itself firmly on the audience: the conquering hero has at last arrived; ceremony and ritual quite rightly underline his triumph. Thus, Simon Norton holds the door 'ceremoniously wide open to allow Harry to enter, with his arm around Jessie, who is carrying a silver cup joyously, rather than reverentially, elevated ...' (p 25). Though descriptions of various productions show Harry elevating the tassie, it should be elevated by Jessie. Since Harry instructs Jessie where to put the tassie, 'under the picture, the picture of the boy that won the final' (p 26), it must be Jessie who is carrying the cup. Jessie, like Susie, functions here, symbolically, as the priestess who attends the altar of the God of War. The stand with Harry's picture is upstage left, which is the area in Act II occupied by the ruined monastery and the priest who chants the Kyrie Eleison. Here is another example of O'Casey's symbolic use of stage space.

In order to intensify further the symbolic symmetry between Acts I and II, the friends on whose shoulders Harry is elevated should appear again, quite recognizably, in the second act: they might be cast as the 2nd and 3rd Soldiers who, together with the rest, 'enter in a close mass ... as if they were almost locked together' (p 3). This 'locking' effect should help to recall their entry in Act I – especially if they enter at stage right beneath the Croucher's platform (or alongside of it) – and so intensify the sense of looking for Harry which the audience must feel. (It would be interesting to try the effect of a tableau scene, both here and in Act I where Harry enters – a tableau scene frozen for a second in time.)

In Act III what kind of flowers does Barney drop on the black quilt covering Harry's bed? Since it is September they cannot be daffodils or tulips, but perhaps they are red and yellow roses. These are the colours of life, of Harry's football uniform; and red is also the colour of sacrifice. The roses, as in Red Roses for Me, suggest the passion of love, as well as all the fine and noble qualities that Harry, ideally, should embody.

After Barney calls attention to the flowers the second time (p 78), perhaps Harry picks up the yellow flowers and flings them beneath the wheels of the Juggernaut.

As he leans on the cross piece and prays, 'God of the miracles, give a poor devil a chance' (p 79), he holds a red rose in his hand.

The flowers should be real flowers, whereas the flowers in Act I should be noticeably artificial.

The correct use of colours in the play is essential to its success onstage. In Act IV the curtains which hang at the entrance to the dance hall are crimson and black (p 80). In the first edition of the play they were crimson and yellow.[6] This change, by itself, shows the meticulous way in which O'Casey revises to achieve the exact symbolic effect. Red and black are, in fact, the principal symbolic colours of the play, with black, the 'colour' of death, predominating over yellow, the colour of life, after Act I.

Harry's suit is not merely dark; it should be black. Harry's 'fantastically shaped' paper hat, symbol of the fool or clown – or of the mock-king who is sacrificed in classical fertility rites – should be red and black.

The lanterns and streamers which decorate the dance hall are many colours, but the streamers which Harry winds around himself and Teddy should be red and black. By contrast, the streamers which encircle Jessie and Barney (p 98) should be all colours, as should the streamers which encircle those who are standing around Harry (p 101).

While black and red, the colours of death and sacrifice, predominate, the 'apple-green casement curtains' (p 80) which are pulled back to allow entrance to the garden, faintly suggest, as do the green of the sycamore trees which replace the poplar trees of Act II, the lost life – the lost Eden – which must be regained.

Music can be used in many scenes as a unifying device. In Act I, even before Harry and Barney leave for the boat, their singing of 'The Silver Tassie' should be accompanied by offstage notes from Conroy's concertina (pp 32–3), which has already been heard just prior to Harry's triumphant entrance (p 25).

Then, in Act II, as an accompaniment to Barney's chorus of 'We're here, because we're here,' mysterious, far-off notes from the concertina may be heard again. (The effect should be something like the mysterious notes of the flute which accompany Ayamonn's dance with Finnoola on the bridge of vision in *Red Roses for Me*.) The music, 'the air of second bar in chorus of "Auld Lang Syne"' (p 39), is that of another nostalgic drinking song. As such, it should help to remind us of Harry as we last saw him at the end of Act I. The unifying effect will be greater, however, if the music we first hear to accompany Harry's entrance in Act I is a medley of 'The Silver Tassie' and 'Auld Lang Syne,' and if the music we hear, just as the singing of 'The Tassie' dies out at the end of Act I, is, again, a few bars of 'Auld Lang Syne.'

In Act II, sharply contrasting the music hall of the concertina, are the 'slow and stately' (p 36) notes of the organ coming from the ruined monastery. The organ music should accompany each of the Croucher's utterances to give the effect of a Black Mass. Later in the act, organ notes might be heard again very briefly to accompany the intoning of the Croucher's 'prayer,' 'Open it at the Psalms and sing that we may be saved from the life and death of the beasts that perish' (p 51). The brassy notes of a church bell, like the one that rings out for Compline at the end of Act III, should also mingle with the organ music here. Then, in Act III, a similar effect might be achieved with bell and organ music as the Sisters sing their hymn 'Salve Regina' and Harry's despairing prayer, 'God of the miracles, give a poor devil a chance' (p 79), cuts across the passionless Latin.

By the third act, notes from the concertina, which by now have become a musical motif for Harry, can be used as a haunting offstage accompaniment to Surgeon Maxwell's naughty song about 'Jess,' and to underline with an even stronger irony the parallel between Surgeon Maxwell flirting with Susie and the flirtatious behaviour of Harry and Jessie that we saw in Act I.

There is still more 'music hall' in Act III in the 'ta-ra-ra-ra' of the dialogue (pp 70, 71). At these moments an offstage trumpet and drum might be lightly heard. With the repetition of 'Sister Peter Alcantara,' the notes of trumpet and drum might grow louder to anticipate their crescendo in the dance hall scene of Act IV.

When these notes are heard again from the dance floor at various intervals during the final act, they carry with them that painful mingling of farce and tragedy which has been growing throughout the play and which reaches a climax in the dance in the wheelchair and in the grotesque fight between Harry and Barney.

In order for Harry's dance in the wheelchair to be a recognizable dance of death, the music from the dance hall must be heard at just the right moments. When Harry calls, 'Trumpets and drum begin!' we should hear the agonizingly bitter-sweet trumpet note, drawn out and held, and the savage beat of the drum. Later, while Harry and Barney fight, these notes echo hauntingly from the dance hall (pp 98, 100), before coming to their finale in the song which ends the play. The fight itself might be stylized since a too realistic portrayal may be too painful for the audience. Try out effects of mime and tableau here, but return always to reality.

Despite what O'Casey says in his Notes to the Stage Version, it would be a shame to omit the song at the end of Act IV. 'Passable' singers must be found and Doctor Maxwell should be one of them. The song is 'belted out' (much like the song 'Keep the 'owme fires burning,' which the Tommies sing as Dublin burns at the end of *The Plough*), and the dance band, with notes of trumpet and drum predominant, crescendoes in a bittersweet agony of pain mingling with joy – more of O'Casey's Ta Ra Ra Boom Dee Ay of life.

Sound effects, a kind of 'electronic' music, can also be used to unify the play. In Act II, for example, a buzzing sound – like the sound of a World War I airplane – might be heard at intervals throughout the 'Bee' scene between the Corporal and the Visitor:

VISITOR   What's that, what was that?
CORPORAL   Wha' was what?
VISITOR   A buzz, I thought I heard a buzz.

CORPORAL A buzz?
VISITOR Of an aeroplane.
CORPORAL Didn't hear. Might have been a bee.
VISITOR No, no; don't think it was a bee. (p 40)

Then, in Act III, where Harry tells Dr Maxwell of the 'buzz' in his legs we should hear, faintly, offstage, the sound of an airplane passing overhead, and, alternately, the buzzing ring of an unanswered telephone. In this way, when the vaudeville of 'Simon and the Telephone' takes place, the 'kind of a buzzing and a roaring noise' (p 86), and 'a thing that's hummin'' (p 87) —sounds that should actually be heard coming from the phone at intervals, especially during the 'Bees' conversation between Sylvester, Simon, and Mrs Foran – may suggest some interesting connections in this otherwise apparently disconnected scene. Though we never do find out who is calling, it should then become clear that the faulty lines of communication extend to Harry's own paralyzed limbs, where there is only 'A timid, faint, fluttering kind of a buzz' (p 68), and to the war zone of Act II.[7]

Of course, not all of these ideas for production may work. But one criterion is essential: everything is 'alive with a strong life.' Whatever tends towards abstraction, towards a symbolic, two-dimensional (even 'one-dimensional') state of being is nonetheless infused with – and buoyed up by – the life which surrounds it.

'RED ROSES FOR ME'

In *Red Roses for Me* the dominant image is the blackshawled Kathleen. Mrs Breydon is the embodiment of a suffering and maternal Ireland, yet, in her, we are also able to glimpse the reality of an ideal Ireland: she is still beautiful, though careworn, and her bearing is as regal as a queen. The thin shawl which she puts on in Act I (p 140) is black, as is the shawl which the Rector arranges around her shoulders at the end of Act IV (p 226).

Eeada, Dympna, and Finnoola, completely enfolded in voluminous black shawls at the beginning of Act III, with only their white faces visible – like three floating wraiths – are grotesque caricatures of the ideal Kathleen. As the Three Fates, they suggest that Ireland's fate is to be a caricature of the ideal. Such a fate is nevertheless transcended on the bridge of vision, where, as their black shawls fall away to reveal 'silvery mantle[s]' (p 199), the three women themselves become embodiments of the ideal Kathleen.

Sheila refuses to play the role of the black-shawled Kathleen: accordingly, she is the only woman in the play who does not wear a black shawl. But, in the final act, she does carry the red roses of Ayamonn's song, and, in this way, her presence may suggest a future for Ireland which can be quite different from her past.

In *Red Roses for Me*, though despair is more fully transcended, the image of crouched and huddled figures, so dominant in *The Tassie*, is also present. In Act III, for example, the men 'lounging' and sitting about the parapets of the bridge should be in noticeably crouched and huddled postures. The contrast between this scene and the end of Act III where the men are standing defiantly, like 'fine bronze statues' (p 199), will then be more striking.

Similarly, the mask-like faces of the men at the beginning of Act III noticeably contrast the faces all 'aglow' in the transfiguration scene. Elements of mime can be experimented with here, and lighting should help, but the effect should not be exaggerated so that it appears completely unrealistic.

In Acts I and II the expressionism should not be ignored (as it usually has been), nor should it be overstated. The most delicate balance between expressionism and realism needs to be maintained.

For instance, in the procession with the statue in Acts I and II the movements should be stylized, but only as stylized as they would be in a real procession or in any other church ritual.

The comic tradition behind these characters is that of the sad clown: they are wearing motley. And yet the mask-like faces are not whiteface as in Beckett, but are deadpan as in a Charlie Chaplin or Buster Keaton movie.

Though in Act I the effect is comic, by the end of the act the scales are tipping towards tragedy. When the statue is returned the hymn is sung 'softly' (p 177). There is no sense of elevation or relief, only sadness. The description of the return of the statue which follows mingles melodrama and comedy: the result is a strong sense of irony and pathos.

In the second act the two railwaymen have a difficult part. On the realistic plane, their mask-like faces and stylized movements appear as awkwardness: 'They stand stock still when they see the Rector' (p 181). But the audience must sense something more: not only a third – but a fourth – dimension. The sudden appearance of the 'half head' (p 181) of Eeada contributes to this effect of unspoken, metaphysical dimensions. Here, again, is a scene from the Absurd.

In Act I Sammy's face is pale as well as mask-like. Try Beckett's whiteface here and see what happens. It may be too much. The Expressionists frequently used spotlights for symbolic effect. Try a spotlight on Sammy.

Sammy's clothing must be brilliantly coloured to contrast the drab tenement surroundings. While Ayamonn is still wearing his bright green silk doublet, the others are in drab trench coats, and Sheila, too, will have put on her fawn-coloured mackintosh 'darkened with heavy rain' (p 139). Sammy's clothes can be oversize to add to the comedy and to help us realize that the 'transformation' in this scene is a false one.

Similarly, the costumes which Ayamonn and Mrs Breydon wear at the beginning of the act should be oversize. Ayamonn's hunchback is bordering on the grotesque. He is, as his mother says, a 'kingly fool' (p 134). The effect of the hunchback in conjunction with Ayamonn's lyrical and 'poetic' speeches is something like the effect of Cyrano de Bergerac's long nose in conjunction with his impassioned love poetry. Pathos and comedy mingle.

The chair which, in Act I, Ayamonn plans to borrow and transform into a 'kingly seat' (p 131) might be incorporated effectively into the stage set of Act II. Ayamonn should sit in it at the table while he counts the shillings he has saved and while he reads from Shakespeare. There might be artificial red roses entwined around the chair.

How should the head of Dunn-Bo appear onstage? It is bathed in light – an image of sacrifice, a symbol of the godhead. And yet it will appear absurd as soon as Ayamonn begins to speak. O'Casey intends both effects to occur almost simultaneously. The success of this scene onstage in Act III depends upon the context which has been built up around the scene from the beginning of the play. If the context up to now has successfully mingled the absurd with the sublime, then this scene should shape itself, almost of its own accord. In other words, the entire play must carry the weight of the interpretation which is demanded here.

Act IV requires great precision in movement and timing. The stage setting is more stylized than has been realized. The chorus must stay outside the iron fence.

When Ayamonn enters he should stand beneath the rowan tree so we may begin to associate it with him, as Mrs Breydon does: 'Stay here, my son, where safety is a green tree with a kindly growth' (p 211).

Perhaps Sheila takes a white blossom from the rowan tree and holds it out to Ayamonn as she pleads with him to stay.

Where booing is heard, followed by 'the rattling fall of a shower of stones' (p 214), add also the sound of glass breaking so that the parallelism with Act II will be more evident.[8]

Try out the effects of having Ayamonn's voice join Brennan's in the final song just as the curtain falls.

If this is effective, then another, more daring device might be tried. If Ayamonn's body is 'covered-up' (p 223) with a black shroud, and the bier is then propped upright in the church, and if the right lighting effect can be achieved, then, when the door to the church is opened for the last time, we might see – as well as hear – the head of Dunn-Bo singing from beyond the grave.

When the curtain rises for the actors to take their curtain call, Ayamonn is in the centre of the stage, the others around him. 'The song all men can sing,' which had momentarily died away at the play's end, crescendoes triumphantly now in the last two stanzas of 'Red Roses for Me.' Thus, the final image presented to the audience by O'Casey's lovely ballad of the Dublin streets will continue to reaffirm our sense of a joyous transfiguration and resurrection.

Notes

INTRODUCTION: BRIDGING THE RIVER OF TIME

1 Quoted in 'Au Revoir to the Abbey Theatre,' a conversation between Sean O'Casey and Barry Fitzgerald in (Mikhail and O'Riordan) *The Sting and the Twinkle* 96. O'Casey himself tells the story to Barry Fitzgerald.
2 Hodson 'O'Casey in Buckinghamshire' *The Sting and the Twinkle* 57
3 *The Sean O'Casey Review* was first published in the fall of 1974. Volume 6 (1981) announces the forthcoming publication of an *O'Casey Annual*, also edited by Robert G. Lowery, to be published by Macmillan (London) in the fall of 1982.
4 O'Casey *Red Roses for Me* III *Collected Plays* (London: Macmillan 1951) 179. All subsequent page references to O'Casey's plays, except where otherwise noted, are from the *Collected Plays* I and II (London: Macmillan 1949) and III and IV (1951) and are made parenthetically in the text.
5 O'Casey 'The Bald Primaqueera (1964)' *Blasts and Benedictions* 73
6 O'Casey 'Behind the Curtained World (1942)' *Blasts and Benedictions* 16

CHAPTER ONE: O'CASEY'S 'HOMEMADE' EXPRESSIONISM: HIS DEBT TO TOLLER

1 Bentley 'The Case of O'Casey,' *What is Theatre?* 26–7. The title, 'A Funny Sort of Red,' is from Bentley's review of the Broadway production of *Red Roses for Me* (December 1955) in which he also discusses O'Casey's communism (pp 265–8).
2 O'Casey 'Green Goddess of Realism' *The Green Crow* 76, 83
3 Foreword *The Green Crow* 15
4 See Hogan, ed. in *Feathers from the Green Crow* 269.

5 Clurman 'Red Roses for Me' 123

6 Allardyce Nicoll describes some of the many kinds of expressionist techniques used by Strindberg and others: 'Short scenes took the place of longer acts, dialogue was made abrupt and given a staccato effect; symbolic (almost morality-type) forms were substituted for "real" characters; realistic scenery was abandoned, and in its place the use of light was freely substituted; frequently choral, or mass, effects were preferred to the employment of single figures, or else single figures were elevated into positions where they became representative of forces larger than themselves.' *World Drama: From Aeschylus to Anouilh* 675. Of course, Strindberg is, properly speaking, a precursor of Expressionism.

7 For example, the American première of *Red Roses*, at the Tributary Theatre of Boston in March 1944, used a very abstract stage design by Matt Horner. This design is reproduced in *Theatre Arts* 28 (July 1944) 437

8 Quoted in De Baun 'Sean O'Casey and the Road to Expressionism' 254

9 Quoted in Rollins 'O'Casey, O'Neill and Expressionism in *The Silver Tassie*' 365. Cf Letter from O'Casey to Rollins, reproduced in Rollins *Sean O'Casey's Drama: Versimilitude and Vision* 118. The irony of this statement, made in the context of O'Casey's comments on *The Silver Tassie*, will become apparent in the following chapter.

10 O'Casey *Sunset and Evening Star* II *Mirror in My House* 144

11 O'Casey, '*The Plough and the Stars* in Retrospect (1960)' *Blasts and Benedictions* 97. Though there are only two pages of holograph material (a note and a page of revisions) for *The Plough and the Stars* in the Berg Collection of the New York Public Library, holographs of *The Tassie* (to take but one example) show that O'Casey began with characters and snatches of dialogue and sometimes with detailed stage settings. Only afterwards did he sketch what might be called 'mini-scenarios' to order the already written scenes within the act. There is no scenario for the entire play even though snatches of dialogue written in the same colour of ink over the same business letter (eg, from Pemberton & Clark, dated 11 November 1927) indicate that he worked simultaneously, for instance, on Act I and Act IV.

12 Though O'Casey's copy of *Masses and Man* is inscribed not only with his name but also with the date – 1924 – O'Casey later denied, both in public statements and private correspondence, that he knew the work of either Strindberg or Toller before he had written *The Silver Tassie*. Either his memory was faulty or he had grown increasingly aware that being linked to Expressionist drama, certainly to Toller, was not likely to make his work, *The Silver Tassie* included, any more popular. For a more complete account of O'Casey's own comments on his indebtedness to Expressionism, the con-

tradictions they contain, and the problems they raise concerning the consciousness of the creative process, see Ayling *Continuity and Innovation* 104–11.

13 O'Casey *Rose and Crown* II *Mirror in My House* 32
14 Templeton 'Sean O'Casey and Expressionism' 47
15 Ibid 50. Italics mine
16 Toller *Man and the Masses* ix. The description of the production is found in Untermeyer's introduction.
17 *Lady Gregory's Journals, 1916–30* 73
18 Massey *A Hundred Different Lives* 87
19 Sean O'Casey, *The Silver Tassie* (1st ed) 42
20 Ayling *Continuity and Innovation* 106. The comment is made in a letter to a student dated 26 November 1957.
21 Although it is a commonplace of O'Casey criticism to refer to Act II of *The Tassie* as a 'Black Mass' – see, for example, Nightingale 'Without Apology' 309 – the fullest implications of this statement have yet to be explored.
22 Templeton 'Sean O'Casey and Expressionism' 50; Kelly 'O'Casey's Near Masterpiece Never Better Handled'
23 Ibid
24 See Massey *A Hundred Different Lives* 83.
25 Gwynn 'Ebb and Flow: Mr O'Casey's Play' 852
26 O'Casey praised Toller's *Seven Plays* in a review article in the *New Statesman*: 'The Thing that Counts' 184, 186.
   Raymond Massey had paid some attention to Toller as well, for he acted in *Masses and Man* (a London Stage Society performance with Sybil Thorndike as Sonia, and Lewis Casson directing) in the spring of 1924, five years before he directed *The Tassie* and about two years after O'Casey would have seen the Dublin Drama League presentation. See Massey *A Hundred Different Lives* 45.
27 See Samuel and Thomas *Expressionism in German Life, Literature and the Theatre* 127.
28 See below 73–5.
29 Toller *Transfiguration* 57. All subsequent page references to the play are from this edition and are made parenthetically in the text.
30 O'Casey 'Immanuel' *Under a Colored Cap* 156
31 Goll 'Two Superdramas' 10–11. In fairness to Toller, it should be added that he was, of course, quite aware of the absurd quality of his work. Unlike O'Casey, however, he was unable to integrate it successfully with pathos and tragedy.
32 W.H. Auden 'In Memory of Ernst Toller' *Collected Shorter Poems, 1930–1944* (London: Faber & Faber 1950) 137

33 Frau Sonja Lerch was one of the principal figures in the Munich uprising of 1919. See Steinhauer *Das Deutsche Drama* II, 99.

34 Toller hanged himself in New York on 22 May 1939 – just a few months before the outbreak of World War II. Compare Toller's statement: 'It is still a question whether we personally exist' (preface to *Man and the Masses* ix), with O'Casey's statement in *Inishfallen, Fare Thee Well*: 'Instead of trying to form Ireland's life, he would shape his own.' II *Mirror in My House* 151

35 Krause *Sean O'Casey: The Man and his Work* 287

CHAPTER TWO: 'THE SILVER TASSIE'

1 *The Letters of Sean O'Casey, 1910–1941* I, 881
2 See Peterson 'Polishing Up the *Silver Tassie* Controversy' 126.
3 *Letters* I, 273
4 Ibid 272
5 Ibid 268
6 J. B.-W. '*The Silver Tassie*,' *New Statesman* 52
7 *Letters* I, 268
8 Jennings '*The Silver Tassie*' 523
9 Massey *A Hundred Different Lives* 91
10 Jennings '*The Silver Tassie*' 523
11 Quoted in Kavanagh *The Story of the Abbey Theatre* 141
12 *Lady Gregory's Journals, 1916–30* 110
13 Leonard 'Aldwych: *The Silver Tassie*' 20
14 Smith 'The Dying God in the Modern Theatre' 270–1
15 Rollins 'O'Casey's *The Silver Tassie*' note 62. Italics mine. Cf Rollins *Sean O'Casey's Drama* 118. The letter is dated 24 March 1960.
16 *Letters* I, 271–2. In *Drums under the Windows* O'Casey records his own stay at St Vincent's Hospital during World War I. There a patient's screams mingle with the 'Hail Mary' of the nuns. There, too, the patients are addressed by number, and the fact that in *The Tassie* he gives his own number, 'Twenty-three,' to the soldier wounded in Flanders again suggests O'Casey's strong identification with, and sympathy for, the sufferings of the soldiers. I *Mirror in My House* 368, 375
17 Leonard 'Aldwych: *The Silver Tassie*' 20
18 O'Casey *Rose and Crown* II *Mirror in My House* 134
19 Ibid 32
20 O'Casey *The Silver Tassie* (1st ed) 28, 29
21 Gwynn 'Ebb and Flow' 851. See also Leonard, 'Aldwych: *The Silver Tassie*' 20, for a picture of the cast with Harry elevated, also reproduced herein.

22 Massey *A Hundred Different Lives* 87
23 In *Drums under the Windows*, O'Casey wrote ironically of his soldier-brother: 'But Tom had never bothered his head about what the word might be. His holy grail was a pint tankard filled to the brim.' II *Mirror in My House* 46
24 Though O'Casey's stage directions read simply, 'Almost opposite the crucifix is a gunwheel to which Barney is tied' (p 35), the 1929 Apollo production, which enjoyed O'Casey's active participation, sets the precedent for having Barney's arms outstretched like the Christ figure opposite. Moreover, three holograph sketches of Act II – in the 45-page holograph notes and draft (11 pp + 34 pp) in the Berg Collection of the New York Public Library – clearly show Barney in this position. See Ayling and Durkan, *O'Casey*, plate 5.
   The 1969 Aldwych production not only followed the Apollo precedent but, at one point in the action, also had the Croucher standing in a cruci-fixion posture on a vertical plane above the gunwheel, thus underlining the parallel fate which has befallen the two soldiers. (For pictures of this production, see Leonard, 'Aldwych' 21, and illustration section in this book.)
25 Letter from O'Casey to Rollins, quoted in 'O'Casey's *The Silver Tassie*.' Cf Rollins *Sean O'Casey's Drama* 118. The letter is dated 24 March 1960.
26 The following is a list of some productions in which the actor who played Teddy doubled as a soldier in Act II (not necessarily the 4th Soldier): the New York City Irish Theatre, October 1929; the Abbey Theatre, Dublin, August 1935; the Nottingham Playhouse, London, April 1967; the Théâtre de L'Est Parisien, Paris, April 1967; the Abbey Theatre, Dublin, September 1972. The following productions are some of those which neglected this doubling: the Interplayers Theatre, Carnegie Hall, New York, July 1949; University of Alberta Studio Theatre, Edmonton, January 1952; the Switzerland Schauspielhaus (German-language première), Zürich, November 1952; the German première in Berlin, June 1953.
27 Massey *A Hundred Different Lives* 83
28 *Letters* I, 268
29 Hogan *The Experiments of Sean O'Casey* 64, 65
30 Krause *Sean O'Casey* 121
31 In the 34-page holograph draft, after the soldiers fall asleep and the head of Barney droops, there is the stage direction: 'Then Corporal Heegan comes around the travers[e] trench followed by the visitor.' Harry is also addressed in the song of the wounded on stretchers: 'Carry on[,] Harry, on to the place of pain.' (This draft was written later than the draft in the holograph notebooks, v.6, where Harry is called 'Jack.') See ill. section.
32 Holograph notebooks, v.6. The notes for Act II at the beginning of this

book contain the earliest setting and the earliest version of the Black Mass. The extensive draft of Act II which follows transposes some of the elements of the setting from the notes, including 'A man kneeling with his head bent under his body,' but leaving behind the legless casualty, since, in any case, the kneeling figure appears 'legless.' As he engages in a ritual which gradually becomes diabolic, his identity keeps changing: from 'The Scholar' to 'The Thinker' – both unrelated to Harry, the soldier who 'has gone to the trenches as unthinkingly as he would go to the polling booth' (p 25) – and, finally, to 'The Croucher.' (See pp [52], [56] – [69] of draft.) See ill.

33 Stamped '"Richard J. Madden play co." From the files of the American play co, inc. Published London, Macmillan 1928.'

34 Hogan *Experiments* 65

35 Despite the clear stage directions (in both the 1928 and 1949 texts) which specify that the soldiers put on their gas masks as the enemy attacks, gas masks are not always worn in production. See, for example, the picture of the German-language première, Zürich, 1952, in *The Sean O'Casey Review* 5 (Fall 1978) 33. In the 34-page holograph draft the importance of the soldiers' wearing the gas masks is stressed when, in the Supplementary order given by the Visitor, 'all units to bring the gas masks,' 'bring' is crossed out and 'wear' is inserted and heavily underlined. See illustration section.

36 *Letters* I, p 235. The letter is dated 5 April 1928. The 1972 Abbey production, for example, cast John Kavanaugh in both roles.

37 Letter from O'Casey to Rollins, reproduced in Rollins' *Sean O'Casey's Drama* 118. See, also, Rollins 'O'Casey, O'Neill and Expressionism in *The Silver Tassie*' 365. The letter is dated 24 March 1960.

38 Massey *A Hundred Different Lives* 83

39 See, for example, Phelan 'The Stage & Screen: A Note on O'Casey' 632. Commenting on the production at the Carnegie Recital Hall, Phelan calls Harry 'a one-dimensional baby from start to finish.'

40 The word 'harry' means to ravage or 'harrow,' as in Christ's harrowing of hell. The manuscripts show O'Casey's preoccupation with finding the exactly right name for a character. Harry Heegan was originally called Jack Travers. (See 41-page early typescript [carbon] drafts, incomplete. Act III, 6.) Moreover, one of the earliest settings for Act II reads, in part: 'A road leads from the right towards the trenches sinking into the ground so that troops marching disappear into the earth. Another leads from the trenches on the left so that men seem to issue from the centre of the earth' (holograph notebooks, v.6, [51]). As the idea of man's involvement in war being a participation in a Black Mass took precedence over the idea of war being a descent into hell, one of the last revisions O'Casey made was to

substitute the Red Cross Station in the ruined monastery for the dug out. In the 34-page holograph draft, however, the earlier setting is described in a way which associates Jack Travers with the soldiers' descent into the centre of the earth, for the trench is described as 'the *travers* trench' (italics mine).

41 In the early typescript (carbon) draft of Act III, after the lights have been put out except for the one near the crucifix, Jack (Harry) 'gripping the hanging bed-support raises himself with an effort [to] a sitting pos[ition].' He then 'turns towards the crucifix and stretches his arms in its direction longingly and appealingly.' In later typescripts the crucifix is replaced by a statue of the Virgin and the bed-support becomes a cross-bar, thus placing Harry, himself, in the position of the crucified Christ, a setting which further parallels the stage setting of Act II (see above, p 31).

Rather than responding to such parallel structures within the realistic framework of the play itself, however, directors of *The Tassie* tend to use more expressionist devices. For example, in his 'Notes on the French Première [25 April 1967] of *The Silver Tassie*' 20–1, Emile Jean Dumay comments that 'the Croucher was to be seen for some time in act 3 in the hospital ward, wearing the same death-mask as in act 2, thus creating an unobtrusive effect of overlapping.' By such non-realistic devices, Guy Retore tries to unify a play in which he sees the second act as 'all but another play in its own right' (p 19).

42 O'Casey's Notes to the Stage Version, as we have seen, specify that the Croucher's ramp should be 'on the left, from view-point of audience' (p 3), that is, at stage right. The November 1969 production at the Aldwych correctly placed Harry's bed at stage right. (There is a picture of Act III of this production, illustrating Hugh Leonard's review, 'Aldwych: *The Silver Tassie*' 23.) Various productions, however, at the discretion of the director and stage designer, have placed Harry's bed in a variety of locations. See Appendix, pp 111–12 for a further discussion of this point.

43 In the early typescript (carbon) draft of Act III organ music originally accompanied the singing of the Salve Regina (p 14).

44 Saros Cowasjee makes this apt comparison. *Sean O'Casey: The Man Behind the Plays* 117.

45 See Appendix, p 113.

46 The 'absurd' quality of *The Tassie*, its cruel mingling of farce and tragedy, is suggested in the 34-page holograph draft by O'Casey's sketch of three heads, each wearing the fool's traditional cap and bells, one of which appears on a stick like a mock sceptre. On the reverse side of this half sheet is Harry's speech from the beginning of Act IV: 'Oh, please your lusty lordship just another – an if I ask a second, smack me well (driving his chair

viciously against Bar[ney].' The crossed-out lines through this speech indicate that it was used in the final draft of the play.

The music hall element of the play is also stronger in the holographs where, in Act IV, prior to taking part in the entertainment, Harry is 'made up like a nigger' with 'Thick red lips ... Goo Goo eyes an all' (11-page holograph notes).

47 *Letters* I, 230. The letter is dated 28 February 1928.

CHAPTER THREE: 'RED ROSES FOR ME'

1 Hogan *The Experiments of Sean O'Casey* 87–8
2 Gellert 'Cold Fry,' 334
3 Aickman 'Mr Sean O'Casey and the Striker' 172
4 '*Red Roses for Me*. 28 December 1955. Booth Theatre,' 15
5 Williams *Drama from Ibsen to Brecht* 153
6 Atkinson *The Sean O'Casey Reader* xvi
7 O'Casey *Drums under the Windows* I *Mirror in My House* 311.
8 That O'Casey did not wish the play to be linked to any one specific historical event is further underlined by his program note written for the production of *Red Roses* at the University of California at Los Angeles in May 1964: 'Though the play is dedicated to the gallant men and women who took part in the long and bitter fight for freedom to join the Union of their choice under the leadership of the great Jim Larkin, the play doesn't deal with that Lockout, but with a strike of Railwaymen of the British Isles long before Jim Larkin was known to any Irish worker.' Quoted in Ayling and Durkan *Sean O'Casey: A Bibliography* 66.

Of course, the number of parallels between the account of the battle in O'Connell Street which O'Casey gives in *Drums under the Windows* (I *Mirror in My House* 290–6) and the action of *Red Roses for Me* reminds us that the 1913 Dublin strike, despite O'Casey's claims to the contrary, is certainly a part of the historical background of the play. The newspaper accounts of the strike in *The New York Times* dated 1 September 1913 (p 6) confirm this conclusion.

9 Krause *Sean O'Casey* 165
10 Ibid
11 See Appendix, p 116.
12 Goll writes: 'We have forgotten entirely that the stage is nothing but a magnifying glass. Great drama had always known this. The Greeks strode on buskins, Shakespeare discoursed with the spirits of dead giants. We have forgotten entirely that the primary symbol of the theatre is the mask. The

mask is rigid, unique, and impressive. It is unchangeable, inescapable; it is Fate. Every man wears his mask, wears what the ancients called his guilt.' 'Two Superdramas' 10.

13 Malone *The Plays of Sean O'Casey* 107

14 *Inishfallen, Fare Thee Well* II *Mirror in My House* 219

15 The most extreme attitude of the Irish Catholic towards the Nelson monument is evidenced by the fact that on 8 March 1966 it was demolished by the IRA. A passage from the autobiographies confirms O'Casey's use of Nelson's Pillar as a symbol of the oppressive might of the state. In *Drums under the Windows*, Sean's account of the violence in O'Connell Street is followed by an imaginary scene on top of Nelson's Pillar in which Bishop Eblananus, St Patrick, and Admiral Nelson carry on a fantastic dialogue. Though St Patrick thinks the disturbance is disgraceful and takes his bishop to task for not keeping his flock in better order, the dialogue ends with St Patrick lashing out at Nelson for the way in which the police have acted: '"Control yourself!" shouted Patrick up at him. "If you could, you wouldn't send your murdherous polis out to maim an' desthroy poor men lookin' for no more than a decent livin'. Gah! If me crozier could only reach up to you, I'd knock your other eye out!"' I *Mirror in My House* 304

16 In *The Silver Tassie*, we recall, the same apt colloquialism is used indiscriminately to refer to both broken dishes and 'broken' soldiers.

17 Matthew 5:3

18 Those members of the audience familiar with the bronze statue erected in the General Post Office in Dublin to commemorate the heroes of the Easter Rising may perhaps catch a glimpse here of a resurrected Cuchulain.

19 Cf Krause *Sean O'Casey* 168.

20 Cf Sean O'Casey *The Drums of Father Ned*, where God is spoken of as 'a shout in the street' (p 92). When asked 'What kind of a shout God could be, 'Michael replies: 'It might be a shout for freedom, like th' shout of men on Bunker Hill; shout of th' people for bread in th' streets, as in th' French Revolution; or for th' world's ownership by th' people, as in th' Soviet Revolution; or it might just be a drunken man, unsteadily meandhering his way home, shouting out Verdi's ... "Oh, Le-on-or-a"' (p 92). Cf James Joyce *Ulysses* (new ed, New York: Modern Library 1961), where Stephen Dedalus also speaks of God as 'a shout in the street' (p 34).

21 Koslow *The Green and the Red* 98

22 As we have seen, this device, which helps to establish and define a symbolic relationship through the use of two clearly delineated, superimposed areas of space onstage, is one O'Casey first used in *The Silver Tassie*. See above, p 29.

23 Cf 2 Peter 1:19.

24 The reference is to Fluther Good in *The Plough and the Stars* 177.

25 Cf Sean O'Casey *Red Roses for Me* (1st ed) 139–41. This restructuring
   occurred after O'Casey saw the 1946 London production at the Embassy
   Theatre. O'Casey also made other revisions to the play which illustrate
   his careful craftsmanship. For example, he shortened Act IV by several
   pages in order to make it more tightly unified, although he had to sacrifice a
   brilliantly comic scene (pp 142–5) to the overall structural demands of the
   play.
   Subsequently, he made still other minor revisions to all four acts. However,
   when preparing *Three More Plays* for publication, he returned to the text of
   the 1951 *Collected Plays*, but added a short scene in Act III in which three
   workmen speak excitedly about the coming meeting and the danger to the
   strikers. Cf *Three More Plays* 281–2.

26 'From *Within the Gates* (1934)' *Blasts and Benedictions* 116

27 In *I Knock at the Door*, O'Casey records, through the eyes of a much younger self, his fascination with the role: 'Johnny watched the little lamplighter
   running, with his little beard wagging, carrying his pole, with a light like a
   sick little star at the top of it, hurrying from lamp to lamp, prodding each
   time a little yellow light into the darkness, till they formed a chain looking
   like a string of worn-out jewels that the darkness had slung round the neck of
   night. His mother returned to the room as he was stretching to see how
   far he could see down the street, and how many of the lights he could count.'
   1 *Mirror in My House* 90

CHAPTER FOUR: A REVALUATION IN THE LIGHT OF
THE ABSURD

1 'The Bald Primaqueera' (1964) *Blasts and Benedictions* 73. The title of the
   article is a burlesque of Ionesco's first play, *The Bald Prima Donna* (called
   The Bald Soprano in North America). The article was completed 21 August
   1964; O'Casey died on 18 September 1964.

2 'Not Waiting for Godot (1956)' *Blasts and Benedictions* 51

3 'The Bald Primaqueera' 73–4

4 Ibid 65. The Theatre of the Absurd shifts, in the 1960s, into the Theatre of
   Cruelty. However, perhaps because an absurd world is also a cruel world,
   we usually end up talking about the same dramatists, such as Ionesco and
   Pinter.

5 *Letters* I, 272

6 'The Bald Primaqueera' 76

7 W.B. Yeats, 'Sailing to Byzantium' *The Collected Poems of W.B. Yeats* (2nd ed, London: Macmillan 1952) 217

8 O'Casey 'The Lark in the Clear Air still sings' *Under a Colored Cap* 135

9 Beckett 'The Essential and the Incidental' 16. This article is a review of O'Casey's *Windfalls*.

10 Krause 'The Principle of Comic Disintegration' 6. Cf Krause *Sean O'Casey* 306.

11 Beckett *Waiting for Godot* 60. All subsequent page references to the play are from this edition and are made parenthetically in the text.

12 Murphy 'Sean O'Casey and "The Bald Primaqueera"' 100. Interestingly enough, however, Murphy comes close to suggesting the same reason I have proposed – the bitterness which O'Casey felt at the rejection of *The Tassie* and the continuing controversy over each subsequent experimental play. In a footnote, Murphy comments on O'Casey's statement that the plays of Pinter and Rudkin '"must be meant for no plays" ... It is hard to know whether O'Casey is using "no" simply to designate plays in which no answers are given, or whether this is a punning comparison with Yeats's Noh plays – which O'Casey never could abide. It is probably both. O'Casey is as much against the theatre of cruelty as he was against Yeats's dance plays during the *Silver Tassie* controversy' (p 110).

13 Artaud *The Theater and Its Double* 79

14 Ibid 8; Murphy 'Sean O'Casey and "The Bald Primaqueera"' 98

15 O'Casey *Inishfallen, Fare Thee Well* II *Mirror in My House* 374

16 Krutch *'Modernism' in Modern Drama* 99

17 Pinter *The Birthday Party* 84–5

18 Artaud *The Theater and Its Double* 13

19 Esslin *The Theatre of the Absurd* 23

20 Beckett *Endgame* 68. All subsequent page references to the play are from this edition and are made parenthetically in the text.

21 Cf Esslin *Theatre of the Absurd* 41. 'Hamm and Clov (ham actor and clown? Hammer and Nail – French "clou"? Nagg = German Nagel; Nell = English: nail also suggests their dependence on Hamm = Hammer).' Beckett would probably delight in all these interpretations and exclude none, but neither would he want us to overlook the obvious: clove is the spice with which ham is traditionally served.

22 See Tynan 'Ionesco: Man of Destiny?' 15.

23 Ionesco 'A Reply to Kenneth Tynan' 14

24 Snowden 'Dialect in the Plays of Sean O'Casey' 387. In the discussion that follows, Snowden's example of the Ulster dialect in *Red Roses* is looked at in the light of the Absurd.

25 By *mise en scène* Artaud means 'everything that occupies the stage, everything that can be manifested and expressed materially on a stage and that is addressed first of all to the senses instead of being addressed primarily to the mind as is the language of words ... This language created for the senses must from the outset be concerned with satisfying them. This does not prevent it from developing later its full intellectual effect on all possible levels and in every direction. But it permits the substitution, for the poetry of language, of a poetry in space which will be resolved in precisely the domain which does not belong strictly to words.' *The Theater and Its Double* 38

26 Murphy 'Sean O'Casey and "The Bald Primaqueera"' 104

27 O'Casey 'Behind the Curtained World (1942)' *Blasts and Benedictions* 16

28 Quoted in Esslin *Theatre of the Absurd* 157. Cf Ionesco 'Discovering the Theatre' 13.

29 Esslin 'The Theatre of the Absurd Reconsidered' 185; Artaud *The Theater and Its Double* 38. Artaud's example of 'humorous poetry in space' is a scene from a Marx Brothers film (p 43).

30 Esslin *Reflections* 185

31 Taylor '*Red Roses for Me*' 66

32 Bentley *Spring's Awakening* 156. Bentley's translation 'stomping' suggests an intriguing possibility: how would this scene appear onstage if it were played in the light of the Absurd?

33 Taylor '*Red Roses for Me*' 66–7

34 O'Casey *Red Roses for Me* (1st ed) 140

35 See above, pp 17–18.

36 Arden *Serjeant Musgrave's Dance* 84

37 Esslin 'Epic Theatre, the Absurd, and the Future' *Reflections* 195. Cf Brandt 'Realism and Parables' 36–40, 49–55.

38 Esslin 'The Theatre of the Absurd Reconsidered,' *Reflections* 186

39 See Esslin 'Epic Theatre, the Absurd, and the Future' *Reflections* 191. 'Any theatre that springs from a fusion of the epic and the absurd will be a *liberated* theatre in the sense of the word in which Tairov, one of its first pioneers, used that term; a theatre in which no holds are barred and in which everything is possible; where realistic décor can alternate with the most fantastic, verse with prose, spoken dialogue with song, musical numbers, and even mime; where the audience can be kept at a distance or drawn into the action, etc.'

40 Cf Murphy 'Sean O'Casey and "The Bald Primaqueera"' 104. 'Is the rooster really so different from Ionesco's rhinoceroses (that the playwright stipulates are to have a certain kind of savage beauty) except that the one is a

symbol of the expansion and liberation of man's humanity while the others represent a loss of humanity?'

41 Kenan 'The Lion' 8–13
42 O'Casey *The Moon Shines on Kylenamoe*, in *Behind the Green Curtains* 145

APPENDIX: NOTES FOR PRODUCTION

1 Cowasjee *Sean O'Casey: The Man Behind the Plays* 122
2 Leonard 'Aldwych: *The Silver Tassie*' 20
3 In correspondence dated 29 June 1981, Raymond Massey writes: 'The soldiers entered in a compact group. It was my idea they should resemble Rodin's sculpture "The Burghers of Calais," not, as O'Casey writes, to suggest weariness, but rather to emphasize their anonymity, their lack of identity.'

In response to my question: 'Did you ever discuss this entrance with O'Casey?' Massey replies: 'Yes, of course.' To an earlier question concerning Massey's elevation of the Croucher, he replies: 'the author was present at rehearsals. As a director, I frequently consulted him and there never was any disagreement.' In response to a question asking if he had ever discussed the doubling of the roles of Harry and the 1st Soldier, Massey replies: 'Of course I did.'

To sum up, what the correspondence confirms is O'Casey's willingness, as an experimental playwright, to try out onstage whatever suggestions the director might make, and, on occasion, even to incorporate into the text those ideas which he felt best served the overall purpose of the play.

4 O'Casey 'Green Goddess of Realism' *The Green Crow* 83
5 In the typescript rejected by the Abbey Theatre (Berg Collection), O'Casey has gone to some trouble to clarify these stage directions by the addition of handwritten revisions. These last-minute revisions are included in the 1928 text of *The Tassie*.
6 O'Casey *The Silver Tassie* (1st edition) 100
7 Cf Williams 'The Unity of The Silver Tassie' 107–8. In a typescript in the Berg Collection, there are two lines of dialogue in which Susie, having taken the phone call, finds it is from someone at the hospital who is enquiring about the state of Harry's health.
8 See above, p 80.

Bibliography

HOLOGRAPHS AND TYPESCRIPTS

O'Casey, Sean Holographs and typescripts of *The Silver Tassie*. Henry W. and
   Albert A. Berg Collection, the New York Public Library (Astor, Lenox, and
   Tilden Foundations), New York

BOOKS

Adamov, Arthur *La grande et la petite manœuvre*, in *Théâtre* I Paris: Gallimard
   1953
Arden, John *Serjeant Musgrave's Dance* New York: Grove Press 1960
Armstrong, William A. *Sean O'Casey* London: Longmans 1967
Artaud, Antonin *The Theater and Its Double* translated by Mary Caroline
   Richards New York: Grove Press 1958
Atkinson, Brooks editor *The Sean O'Casey Reader: Plays, Autobiographies, Opinions*
   New York: St Martin's Press 1968
Ayling, Ronald *Continuity and Innovation in Sean O'Cassey's Drama: A Critical
   Monograph* Salzburg Studies in English Literature, no 23 Salzburg: Institut für
   Englische Sprache und Literatur 1976
– editor *Sean O'Casey: Modern Judgements* London: Macmillan 1969
– and Michael J. Durkan *Sean O'Casey: A Bibliography* London: Macmillan
   1978
Beckett, Samuel *Endgame* New York: Grove press 1958
– *Waiting for Godot* New York: Grove Press 1954
Benstock, Bernard *Paycocks and Others: Sean O'Casey's World* Dublin: Gill and
   Macmillan 1975
– *Sean O'Casey* Lewisburg: Bucknell University Press, 1970

Bentley, Eric translator and editor *Spring's Awakening* by Frank Wedekind VI
   The Modern Theatre Garden City NY: Doubleday Anchor Books 1960
– *What is Theatre? Incorporating the Dramatic Event and Other Reviews,
   1944–1967* New York: Atheneum 1968
Brandt, G.W. 'Realism and Parables: from Brecht to Arden' in *Contemporary
   Theatre* edited by John Russell Brown and Bernard Harris. London: Edward
   Arnold (Publishers) Ltd 1962, pp 33–55
Cowasjee, Saros *O'Casey* Edinburgh: Oliver & Boyd 1966
– *Sean O'Casey: The Man behind the Plays* Edinburgh: Oliver & Boyd 1963
Da Rin, Doris *Sean O'Casey* World Dramatist Series. New York: Frederick
   Ungar 1976
Esslin, Martin *The Theatre of the Absurd* Revised edition. Garden City NY:
   Doubleday Anchor Books 1969
– 'The Theatre of the Absurd Reconsidered' in *Reflections: Essays on Modern
   Theatre* Garden City NY: Doubleday Anchor Books 1971
Fallon, Gabriel *Sean O'Casey: The Man I Knew* Boston: Little, Brown & Co.
   1965
Frayne, John P. *Sean O'Casey* Columbia Essays on Modern Writers. New
   York: Columbia University Press 1976
Goldstone, Herbert *In Search of Community: The Achievement of Sean
   O'Casey* Cork: Mercier Press 1972
Goll, Yvan 'Two Superdramas' translated and introduced by Walter H. Sokel
   in *An Anthology of German Expressionist Drama* Garden City NY: Doubleday
   Anchor Books 1963, pp 9–11
Gregory, Augusta *Lady Gregory's Journals, 1916–30* edited by Lennox Robin-
   son. London: Putnam, & Co 1946
Hogan, Robert *After the Irish Renaissance: A Critical History of the Irish Drama
   since 'The Plough and the Stars'* Minneapolis: University of Minnesota Press 1967
– *The Experiments of Sean O'Casey* New York: St Martin's Press 1960
Kavanagh, Peter *The Story of the Abbey Theatre* New York: The Devin-Adair Co
   1950
Kilroy, Thomas, editor *Sean O'Casey: A Collection of Critical Essays* Englewood
   Cliffs NJ: Prentice-Hall 1975
Koslow, Jules *The Green and the Red: Sean O'Casey, the Man and His Plays* New
   York: Golden Griffin Books 1950
Krause, David *Sean O'Casey: The Man and His Work* Enlarged edition. New York:
   Macmillan 1975
– *Sean O'Casey and His World* London: Thames and Hudson 1976
Krutch, Joseph Wood '*Modernism' in Modern Drama* Ithaca: Cornell Univer-
   sity Press 1953

2

Malone, Maureen *The Plays of Sean O'Casey* Carbondale: Southern Illinois University Press, 1969

Margulies, Martin B. *The Early Life of Sean·O'Casey* Dublin: Dolmen Press 1970

Massey, Raymond *A Hundred Different Lives* Toronto: McClelland and Stewart 1979

Mikhail, E.H. *Sean O'Casey: A Bibliography of Criticism* Seattle: University of Washington Press 1972

– and John O'Riordan editors *The Sting and the Twinkle: Conversations with Sean O'Casey* London: Macmillan 1974

Nicoll, Allardyce *World Drama: From Aeschylus to Anouilh* 2nd edition, revised and enlarged; London: George G. Harrap 1976

O'Casey, Eileen *Eileen* edited and introduced by J.C. Trewin. New York: St Martin's Press 1976

– *Sean* edited and introduced by J.C. Trewin. New York: Coward, McCann & Geoghegan 1972

O'Casey, Sean *Behind the Green Curtains; Figuro in the Night; The Moon Shines on Kylenamoe* London: Macmillan 1961

– *The Bishop's Bonfire* London: Macmillan 1955

– *Blasts and Benedictions: Articles and Stories* edited by Ronald Ayling. London: Macmillan 1967

– *Collected Plays* 4 volumes. London: Macmillan 1949–51

– *The Drums of Father Ned* New York: St Martin's Press 1960

– *Feathers from the Green Crow: Sean O'Casey, 1905–1925* edited by Robert Hogan. Columbia: University of Missouri Press 1962

– *The Flying Wasp* London: Macmillan 1937

– *The Green Crow* London: W.H. Allen 1957

– *The Harvest Festival* New York: The New York Public Library (Astor, Lenox and Tilden Foundations) & Readex Books 1979

– *The Letters of Sean O'Casey* I *1910–1941* edited by David Krause. New York: Macmillan 1975

– *The Letters of Sean O'Casey* II *1942–1954* edited by David Krause. New York: Macmillan 1980

– *Mirror in My House: The Autobiographies of Sean O'Casey* 2 volumes. New York: Macmillan 1956

– *Red Roses for Me* 1st edition. London: Macmillan 1942

– *The Silver Tassie* 1st edition. London: Macmillan 1928

– *Three More Plays by Sean O'Casey: The Silver Tassie, Purple Dust, Red Roses for Me* introduced by J.C. Trewin. London: Macmillan 1965

– *Under a Colored Cap: Articles Merry and Mournful with Comments and a Song* London: Macmillan 1963

138 Bibliography

Pinter, Harold *The Birthday Party* Revised edition. London: Methuen 1965
Rollins, Ronald Gene *Sean O'Casey's Drama: Verisimilitude and Vision* University AL: University of Alabama Press 1979
Samuel, Richard, and R. Hinton Thomas *Expressionism in German Life, Literature and the Theatre (1910–1924)* Cambridge: W. Heffer & Sons 1939
Scrimgeour, James R. *Sean O'Casey* Boston: Twayne Publishers 1978
Smith, B.L. *O'Casey's Satiric Vision* Kent, Ohio: Kent State University Press 1978
Steinhauer, H. editor *Das Deutsche Drama, 1880–1933* II. New York: W.W. Norton & Co. Inc. 1938
Thompson, William Irwin 'The Naturalistic Image: O'Casey,' *The Imagination of an Insurrection: Dublin, Easter 1916: A Study of an Ideological Movement* New York: Oxford University Press 1967
Toller, Ernst *Man and the Masses* translated by Louis Untermeyer. New York: Doubleday, Page & Co. 1924
– *Transfiguration* translated by Edward Crankshaw; *Masses and Man* translated by Vera Mendel in *Seven Plays* New York: Liveright Publishing Corp. nd
Williams, Raymond *Drama from Ibsen to Brecht* London: Chatto & Windus 1968
– *Drama from Ibsen to Eliot* London: Chatto & Windus 1952

PERIODICALS

Ayling, Ronald 'Sean O'Casey and the Abbey Theatre, Dublin' *Dalhousie Review* 52 (spring 1972) 21–33
Cowasjee, Saros 'The Juxtaposition of Tragedy and Comedy in the Plays of Sean O'Casey' *Wascana Review* 2 (spring-summer 1967) 75–89
De Baun, Vincent C. 'Sean O'Casey and the Road to Expressionism' *Modern Drama* 4 (December 1961) 254–9
Doyle, Jaqueline 'Liturgical Imagery in Sean O'Casey's *The Silver Tassie*' *Modern Drama* 2 (March 1978) 29–38
Dumay, Emile Jean 'Notes on the French Première of *The Silver Tassie*' *Sean O'Casey Review* 5 (fall 1978) 19–21
Durbach, Errol 'Peacocks and Mothers: Theme and Dramatic Metaphor in O'Casey's *Juno and the Paycock*' *Modern Drama* 15 (May 1972) 15–25
Esslinger, Pat M. 'Sean O'Casey and the Lockout of 1913: *Materia Poetica* of the Two Red Plays' *Modern Drama* 6 (May 1963) 53–63
Harmon, Maurice, editor *Irish University Review* 10 (spring 1980). This is a special issue, *Sean O'Casey: Roots & Branches*, edited by Christopher Murray.
Hogan, Robert 'The Haunted Inkbottle: A Preliminary Study of Rhetorical Devices in the Late Plays of Sean O'Casey' *James Joyce Quarterly* 8 (fall 1970) 76–95

– 'O'Casey's Dramatic Apprenticeship' *Modern Drama* 4 (December 1961) 243-53

Ionesco, Eugène 'Discovering the Theatre' translated by Leonard C. Pronko *Tulane Drama Review* 4 (September 1959)

Kenan, Amos 'The Lion' translated by Rosette Lamont *First Stage, A Quarterly of New Drama* 4 (spring 1965) 8–13

Kosok, Heinz 'The Revision of *The Silver Tassie*' *Sean O'Casey Review* 5 (fall 1978) 15–18

Krause, David 'The Principle of Comic Disintegration' *James Joyce Quarterly* 8 (fall 1970) 3–12

– 'Sean O'Casey: 1880–1964' *Massachusetts Review* 6 (winter-spring 1965) 233–51

Lowery, Robert G. 'O'Casey, Critics and Communism' *Sean O'Casey Review* 1 (fall 1974) 14–18

Malone, Maureen '*Red Roses for Me:* Fact and Symbol' *Modern Drama* 9 (September 1966) 147–52

McHugh, Roger 'Counterparts: Sean O'Casey and Samuel Beckett' *Moderna Sprak* 67 (1973) 217–22

Murphy, R[obert] Patrick 'Sean O'Casey and the Avant-Garde' *Colby Library Quarterly* 11 (December 1975) 235–48

– 'Sean O'Casey and "The Bald Primaqueera"' *James Joyce Quarterly* 8 (fall 1970) 96–110

Peterson, Richard F. 'Polishing Up the *Silver Tassie* Controversy: Some Lady Gregory and W.B. Yeats Letters to Lennox Robinson' *Sean O'Casey Review* 4 (spring 1978) 121–9

Rollins, Ronald G. 'O'Casey, O'Neill and Expressionism in *The Silver Tassie*' *Bucknell Review* 10 (May 1962) 364–9

– 'O'Casey's *The Silver Tassie*' *Explicator* 20 (April 1962) item 62

– 'Pervasive Patterns in *The Silver Tassie*' *Eire-Ireland* 6 (winter 1971) 29–37

Smith, Winifred 'The Dying God in the Modern Theatre' *Review of Religion* 5 (March 1941) 264–75

Snowden, J.A. 'Dialect in the Plays of Sean O'Casey' *Modern Drama* 14 (February 1972) 387–91

Templeton, Joan 'Sean O'Casey and Expressionism' *Modern Drama* 14 (May 1971) 47–62

Williams, Simon 'The Unity of *The Silver Tassie*' *Sean O'Casey Review* 4 (spring 1978) 99–112

REVIEWS AND NEWSPAPER ARTICLES

Aickmann, Robert Fordyce 'Mr Sean O'Casey and the Striker. *Red Roses for Me*: Embassy, Swiss Cottage' *Nineteenth Century* 139 (April 1946) 172–5

B.-W., J. *'The Silver Tassie' New Statesman* 34 (19 October 1929) 52–3

Beckett, Samuel 'The Essential and the Incidental' *Bookman* 86 (December 1934) 16

Clurman, Harold *'Red Roses for Me' Nation* 182 (14 January 1956) 39–40. Reprinted in *Lies Like Truth* New York: Macmillan 1958

Coughlan, Aileen 'All-Ireland Drama Festival' *Irish Times* 30 April 1968, p 10

– 'Amateur Drama' *Irish Times* 31 May 1968, p 10

– 'Athlone Festival: O'Casey' *Irish Times* 6 May 1968, p 10

Gascoigne, Bamber 'Meccano Drama: *Red Roses for Me* (Mermaid)' *Spectator* 209 (14 September 1962) 364

Gellert, Roger 'Cold Fry' *New Statesman* 64 (14 September 1962) 334

Gwynn, Stephen 'Ebb and Flow: Mr O'Casey's Play' *Fortnightly Review* 126 (2 December 1929) 851–3

Hewes, Henry 'Sean O'Casey's One-Shilling Opera' *Saturday Review of Literature* 39 (14 January 1956) 20

'Huzzas for O'Casey: *Red Roses for Me*: Produced by Gordon W. Pollock. Directed by John O'Shaughnessy' *Newsweek* 47 (9 January 1956) 44–5

Ionesco, Eugène 'A Reply to Kenneth Tynan: The Playwright's Role' *Observer* (29 June 1958) 14

Jennings, Richard *'The Silver Tassie* by Sean O'Casey: At the Apollo Theatre' *Spectator* 143 (19 October 1929) 523

Kelly, Seamus 'O'Casey's Near Maserpiece Never Better Handled' *Irish Times* (27 September 1972)

– *'Red Roses for Me* at the Abbey' *Irish Times* (August 1967) 8

Leonard, Hugh 'Aldwych: *The Silver Tassie' Plays and Players* 17 (November 1969) 20–3

MacCarthy, Desmond 'Very Much on the Spot' *New Statesman* 35 (17 May 1930) 180–1

Nightingale, Benedict 'Without Apology' *New Statesman* 78 (19 September 1969) 390

O'Casey, Sean 'The Thing that Counts' *New Statesman* 9 (9 February 1935) 184, 186. A review of Toller's *Seven Plays*

Phelan, Kappo 'The Stage & Screen: A Note on O'Casey' *Commonweal* 50 (7 October 1949) 632

Redfern, James *'Red Roses for Me*: At the Embassy Theatre' *Spectator* 176 (8 March 1946) 244

'The Silver Tassie: Scene from the German-language première, Zurich, 1952' *Sean O'Casey Review* 5 (fall 1978) 33

'Red Roses for Me. 28 December 1955. Booth Theatre' *Theatre Arts* 40 (March 1956) 15

'*Red Roses for Me*: Design by Matt Horner' *Theatre Arts* 28 (July 1944) 437

'*Red Roses for Me*: Olympia Theatre, Dublin' *Theatre Arts* 27 (October 1943) 586

Stokes, Sewell 'New Plays at Last! The English Spotlight: *Red Roses for Me*' *Theatre Arts* 30 (June 1946) 355–6

Taylor, John Russell '*Red Roses for Me*' *Plays and Players* 10 (November 1962) 66–7

Tynan, Kenneth 'Ionesco, Man of Destiny?' *Observer* (22 June 1958) 15

– 'Theatre. Second Lap: *Red Roses for Me* (Mermaid)' *Observer* (9 September 1962) 22

Index

L5